The Bail Reform Act of 1984
Third Edition

David N. Adair, Jr.

Federal Judicial Center 2006

This Federal Judicial Center publication was undertaken in furtherance of the Center's statutory mission to develop and conduct education programs for the judicial branch. The views expressed are those of the author and not necessarily those of the Federal Judicial Center.

Blank pages inserted to preserve pagination when printing double-sided copies.

Contents

Preface vii

I. Pretrial Release 1
   A. Release on Personal Recognizance 1
   B. Conditional Release 1
   C. Written Findings 4
   D. Advising Defendant of Penalty 4

II. Pretrial Detention 5
   A. Statutory Grounds 5
   B. Constitutionality 5
   C. Factors To Be Considered 6
   D. Standard of Proof 8
   E. Definition of Dangerousness 8
   F. Detention Hearing 9
      1. Statutory Requirements 9
      2. Timing of Detention Motion and Hearing 11
         a. Statutory requirement; remedy for a violation 11
         b. Continuances 13
         c. Waiver by defendant 15
   G. Rebuttable Presumptions 16
      1. The Two Presumptions 16
      2. Application of "Drug-and-Firearm-Offender Presumption" 16
         a. Ten-year maximum charge required 16
         b. Probable cause and grand jury indictments 17
         c. Formal charge required 17
         d. Effect of presumption 18
         e. Constitutionality 19
   H. Temporary Detention 20
   I. Detention Upon Review of a Release Order 21
   J. Evidence and Right to Counsel 22
      1. Right to Counsel 22
      2. Hearsay Evidence 22

3. Proffer Evidence 23
   4. Cross-Examination 23
   5. Ex Parte Evidence 24
   6. Challenged Evidence 25
   7. Electronic Surveillance 25
   8. Psychiatric Examination 25
 K. Hearings Involving Multiple Defendants 26
 L. Written Findings 26

III. The Crime Victims' Rights Act of 2004 27

IV. Modification of Detention Order 28
 A. Changed Circumstances 28
 B. Length of Detention 28

V. Revocation and Modification of Release 31
 A. Revocation for Violation of Release Conditions 31
 B. Modification or Revocation Where Defendant Has Not Violated Release Conditions 32

VI. Review by the District Judge 33

VII. Review by the Court of Appeals 34

VIII. Release or Detention Pending Sentence 36

IX. Release or Detention Pending Appeal 38
 A. Release Requirements 38
 B. Definitions of "Substantial Question" and "Likely" 41
 C. "Exceptional Reasons" 42

X. Release or Detention of a Material Witness 43

XI. Release or Detention Pending Revocation of Probation or Supervised Release 44

XII. Offense Committed While on Bail 44

XIII. Sanctions 47
 A. Failure to Appear 47
 B. Contempt 48

XIV. Credit Toward Detention 48

For Further Reference 51

Appendix A: The Bail Reform Act of 1984, 18 U.S.C. §§ 3141–3150, 3156 53

Appendix B: The Sentencing Reform Act of 1984, Selected Provision: 18 U.S.C. § 3585 69

Table of Cases 71

Blank pages inserted to preserve pagination when printing double-sided copies.

Preface

The first edition of this monograph, published in 1987, was written by Deirdre Golash of the Federal Judicial Center. It was updated in a 1993 second edition by Alan Hirsch and Diane Sheehey of the Center. Much of the case law since then follows the principles established in the cases referenced in the second edition and often simply cites to those cases. In this third edition, David N. Adair, Jr., former associate general counsel of the Administrative Office of the United States Courts, primarily addresses areas that have been changed by statute or case law since the second edition, and elsewhere cites more recent cases that discuss the substantive issues. This edition includes case law through June 1, 2006.

The Bail Reform Act of 1984 (18 U.S.C. §§ 3141–3150) authorizes and sets forth the procedures for a judicial officer to order the release or detention of an arrested person pending trial, sentence, and appeal.

The Bail Reform Act of 1984 has been amended several times. References in this monograph to the "Bail Reform Act" or the "Act" are to the amended version in effect as of October 30, 2005, and all cites to the U.S. Code are to the most current version in effect at the time of this printing.

Appendix A reproduces the Bail Reform Act of 1984, as amended, as of October 30, 2005. Appendix B sets forth a selected provision of the Sentencing Reform Act of 1984.

Blank pages inserted to preserve pagination when printing double-sided copies.

I. Pretrial Release

A. Release on Personal Recognizance

Under 18 U.S.C. § 3142(b), the defendant must be released on personal recognizance or unsecured personal bond unless the judicial officer[1] determines "that such release will not reasonably assure the appearance of the person as required or will endanger the safety of any other person or the community." Release is always subject to the mandatory condition "that the person not commit a Federal, State, or local crime during the period of release."[2]

B. Conditional Release

Under section 3142(c), if the judicial officer determines that release of a defendant on personal recognizance or unsecured bond presents a risk of the defendant's nonappearance or a danger to any person or to the community, the judicial officer may impose additional conditions of release. The judicial officer must choose "the least restrictive . . . condition, or combination of conditions, that . . . will reasonably assure the appearance of the person as required and the safety of any other person and the community."[3]

The statute includes a list of thirteen possible conditions of release that courts may impose in appropriate cases; it also empowers courts to impose "any other condition that is reasonably necessary" to ensure appearance and protect the community.[4] Release conditions must be relevant to the purposes of ensuring appearance and safety.[5] Various

---

1. Unless otherwise noted in a specific provision of the Act, a "judicial officer" may be a federal appellate, district, or magistrate judge; a state judge, justice, magistrate, or justice of the peace; or a city mayor. 18 U.S.C. §§ 3156(a), 3041; Fed. R. Crim. P. 1(b)(3).
2. 18 U.S.C. § 3142(b), (c)(1)(A).
3. *Id.* § 3142(c)(1)(B).
4. *Id.* § 3142(c)(1)(B)(xiv).
5. United States v. Goosens, 84 F.3d 697, 702 (4th Cir. 1996) (it was error to impose a condition prohibiting cooperation with law enforcement officers without a finding that such a

conditions that district courts have imposed under the catchall provision of the statute include drug testing, house arrest, submission to warrantless searches,[6] telephone monitoring, residence in a halfway house, electronic bracelet monitoring, freezing of defendant's assets,[7] limiting access to the Internet and computers,[8] and submission to random, unannounced visits by pretrial services officers.

Several courts have stated that conditions of release vary with the circumstances of each case and should be based on an individual evaluation of the defendant; the treatment of other defendants is generally not relevant.[9]

---

condition was necessary for the particular defendant); United States v. Vargas, 925 F.2d 1260, 1265 (10th Cir. 1991) (same); United States v. French, 900 F.2d 1300, 1302 (8th Cir. 1990) (same); United States v. Brown, 870 F.2d 1354, 1358 n.5 (7th Cir. 1989) (it was error to require defendant either to accept court-appointed counsel or to remain in forum district; although it might be permissible to require retention of counsel as a condition of release if necessary to ensure safety of the community or appearance at trial, the magistrate judge did it "in order to ensure a fair and orderly trial. Although laudable in spirit, such concerns do not have . . . roots in the Bail Reform Act."); United States v. Rose, 791 F.2d 1477, 1480 (11th Cir. 1986) (condition that bail bond be retained by the clerk to pay any fine imposed on defendant was irrelevant to purpose of ensuring appearance and thus violated Eighth Amendment prohibition on excessive bail). Note that 28 U.S.C. § 2044 authorizes the court to require a bond to be applied toward payment of a criminal financial penalty, *United States v. Frazier*, 772 F.2d 1451, 1452–53 (9th Cir. 1985) (per curiam) (condition that property securing bond be unencumbered held improper because it was geared more toward protecting government's property interest than ensuring defendant's appearance).

6. United States v. Kills Enemy, 3 F.3d 1201, 1203 (8th Cir. 1993), *cert. denied*, 510 U.S. 1138 (1994) (search of defendant awaiting sentencing valid pursuant to warrantless search condition). *Cf.* United States v. Scott, 450 F.3d 863 (9th Cir. 2006) (drug test pursuant to warrantless search condition must be supported by probable cause, though court cautioned that it does not intend to establish categorical prohibition on drug-testing bail conditions).

7. *See* United States v. Welsand, 993 F.2d 1366 (8th Cir. 1993).

8. *Cf.* United States v. Johnson, 446 F.3d 272 (2d Cir. 2006) (upholding supervised release condition restricting computer use). Though the imposition of restrictions on computer use and access to computers in supervised release and probation contexts may involve different considerations than in the pretrial release context, the opinion in *Johnson* may be helpful to judges considering these kinds of conditions in appropriate pretrial situations.

9. *See* United States v. Patriarca, 948 F.2d 789, 794 (1st Cir. 1991) (noting "error of lumping defendants together" and rejecting government's argument that because defendant is a member of the same organized crime family as another detainee he should be "painted with the same brush and merit[s] the same treatment"); United States v. Tortora, 922 F.2d 880, 888 (1st Cir. 1990) (rejecting defendant's contention that he should be treated the same as his confederates: "Detention determinations . . . must be based on the evidence which is before the court regarding the particular defendant. . . . The inquiry is factbound. No two defendants are likely

Section 3142(c)(2) precludes a judicial officer from "impos[ing] a financial condition that results in the pretrial detention of the person." This provision does not require bail to be set at a figure that the defendant can readily post: "a court must be able to induce a defendant to go to great lengths to raise the funds without violating the condition in § 3142(c)."[10] Even if the defendant cannot afford the bail amount, the condition may not run afoul of the statute.[11] Courts have held that section 3142(c)(2) prevents only the "'sub rosa use of money bond' to detain defendants whom the court considers dangerous."[12] Thus, although a court cannot intentionally detain the defendant by setting bail at an unaffordable level, it may set bail at whatever level it finds reasonably necessary to secure appearance; if the defendant cannot afford that amount, the defendant is detained not because he or she "cannot raise the money, but because without the money, the risk of flight is too great."[13] However, courts of appeals have held that if the defendant informs the trial court that he or she cannot make bail, the trial court "must explain its reasons for determining that the particular requirement is an indispensable component of the conditions for release."[14]

If the defendant does post bail, but there are grounds to suspect that the source of funds offered is illegitimate, the court may hold a hearing to inquire into the matter.[15]

---

to have the same pedigree or to occupy the same position."); United States v. Spilotro, 786 F.2d 808, 816 (8th Cir. 1986) (applying same condition of release to all defendants in district was abuse of discretion).

10. United States v. Szott, 768 F.2d 159, 160 (7th Cir. 1985) (per curiam) ($1 million bail upheld).

11. United States v. Mantecon-Zayas, 949 F.2d 548, 550 (1st Cir. 1991); United States v. McConnell, 842 F.2d 105, 108–10 (5th Cir. 1988) (en banc); United States v. Wong-Alvarez, 779 F.2d 583, 584 (11th Cir. 1985) (per curiam); United States v. Jessup, 757 F.2d 378, 388–89 (1st Cir. 1985).

12. *Mantecon-Zayas*, 949 F.2d at 551 (quoting S. Rep. No. 98-225, at 16 (1983)), *reprinted in* 1984 U.S.C.C.A.N. 3182, 3199.

13. *Jessup*, 757 F.2d at 389.

14. *Mantecon-Zayas*, 949 F.2d at 551. *Accord McConnell*, 842 F.2d at 110. *Cf. Szott*, 768 F.2d at 160 (defendant's bare assertion that he could not post $1 million bail did not rebut government's assertion that the defendant may be able to raise the money).

15. *See, e.g.*, United States v. O'Brien, 895 F.2d 810, 817 (1st Cir. 1990) (district court erred in finding that "it was precluded from conducting a hearing once the set condition had been met"); United States v. Nebbia, 357 F.2d 303, 304 (2d Cir. 1966) (seminal case suggesting a hearing).

C. Written Findings

Federal Rule of Appellate Procedure 9(a) requires that a written statement of reasons accompany a release order.[16] In several circuits, a failure to comply with this requirement in contested cases results in a remand.[17] Section 3142(h)(1) specifies that a release order must set forth the conditions of release in a "clear and specific" manner. Some courts have, in the context of an order of detention, permitted transcribed oral findings and reasons to satisfy the similar requirements of 18 U.S.C. § 3142(i).[18]

The statement of reasons should not be perfunctory. For example, where a district court stated that listed conditions of release "will reasonably assure the safety of the community," the First Circuit remanded because this "conclusory language accomplished very little in the way of finding subsidiary facts or furnishing needed enlightenment to an appellate tribunal. The judge gave no explanation of why he believed the proposed conditions would prove adequate."[19]

D. Advising Defendant of Penalty

At the time of the defendant's release, the judicial officer must also advise the person of the penalty and consequences of violating a term of release.[20] The Fifth Circuit held that it is not sufficient to inform the defendant that a violation of release conditions will result in arrest; the judicial officer must advise the defendant of the penalty for the violation: a term of imprisonment under section 3147.[21]

---

16. Fed. R. App. P. 9(a) ("Upon an entry of an order refusing or imposing conditions of release, the district court shall state in writing the reasons for the action taken.").
17. United States v. Blasini-Lluberas, 144 F.3d 881 (1st Cir. 1998); United States v. Swanquist, 125 F.3d 573, 575 (7th Cir. 1997) (per curiam), *cert. denied,* 526 U.S. 1160 (1999); United States v. Cantu, 935 F.2d 950, 951 (8th Cir. 1991); United States v. Tortora, 922 F.2d 880, 883 (1st Cir. 1990); United States v. Wheeler, 795 F.2d 839, 841 (9th Cir. 1986); United States v. Hurtado, 779 F.2d 1467, 1480 (11th Cir. 1985); United States v. Coleman, 777 F.2d 888, 892 (3d Cir. 1985).
18. United States v. Peralta, 849 F.2d 625, 626 (D.C. Cir. 1988); United States v. Davis, 845 F.2d 412, 415 (2d Cir. 1988).
19. *Tortora,* 922 F.2d at 883.
20. 18 U.S.C. § 3142(h)(2).
21. United States v. Onick, 889 F.2d 1425, 1433–34 (5th Cir. 1989).

II. Pretrial Detention

A. *Statutory Grounds*

The judicial officer must order the defendant detained if no condition will reasonably ensure the appearance of the defendant and the safety of the community.[22] Thus, it appears that a showing of either the defendant's likelihood to flee or dangerousness to others requires detention. Courts have operated on this assumption, and a number have made it explicit.[23]

The court must consider all reasonable, less-restrictive alternatives to detention.[24] The First Circuit cautions that the Act "does not require release of a dangerous defendant if the only combination of conditions that would reasonably assure societal safety consists of heroic measures beyond those which can fairly be said to have been within Congress's contemplation."[25] At the same time, courts have recognized that "[p]retrial detention is still an exceptional step,"[26] and the Eighth Circuit has noted that "reasonably assure" does not mean "guarantee."[27]

B. *Constitutionality*

Even before the Bail Reform Act of 1984 was enacted, the Supreme Court had upheld the constitutionality of detention based on likelihood of flight.[28] In *United States v. Salerno*,[29] the Court upheld the Act

---

22. 18 U.S.C. § 3142(e).

23. United States v. King, 849 F.2d 485, 488 (11th Cir. 1988); United States v. Ramirez, 843 F.2d 256, 257 (7th Cir. 1988); United States v. Sazenski, 806 F.2d 846, 848 (8th Cir. 1986) (per curiam); United States v. Fortna, 769 F.2d 243, 249 (5th Cir. 1985).

24. 18 U.S.C. § 3142(e). *See* United States v. Infelise, 934 F.2d 103, 105 (7th Cir. 1991) (remanding because defendants proposed electronic surveillance anklets rather than detention, and trial court failed to consider whether it was a reasonable alternative).

25. United States v. Tortora, 922 F.2d 880, 887 (1st Cir. 1990) (rejecting claim that house arrest with twenty-four-hour surveillance was in order).

26. United States v. Torres, 929 F.2d 291, 292 (7th Cir. 1991) (citing United States v. Salerno, 481 U.S. 739, 749 (1987)). *Accord* United States v. Townsend, 897 F.2d 989, 994 (9th Cir. 1990) ("Only in rare cases should release be denied.").

27. United States v. Orta, 760 F.2d 887, 891–92 (8th Cir. 1985) (en banc).

28. Bell v. Wolfish, 441 U.S. 520, 533–34 (1979).

29. 481 U.S. 739 (1987).

itself against the claim that detention based on the defendant's dangerousness violates due process. The Court, however, "intimate[d] no view as to the point at which detention in a particular case might become excessively prolonged"[30] and thus constitute a violation of due process. Appellate courts since *Salerno* have held that due process challenges to pretrial detention must be decided on a case-by-case basis. The relevant cases are discussed in Part III, *infra*.

C. Factors To Be Considered

Section 3142(g) sets forth the factors for the judicial officer to consider in determining whether to release the defendant. These factors must be considered whenever release is sought, whether under section 3142 (pending trial), section 3143 (pending appeal or sentence), section 3144 (material witness), or section 3148(b) (violation of release condition).[31] The factors are

(1) the nature and circumstances of the offense charged, including whether the offense is a crime of violence or involves a narcotic drug;
(2) the weight of the evidence against the person;
(3) the history and characteristics of the person, including—
   (A) the person's character, physical and mental condition, family ties, employment, financial resources, length of residence in the community, community ties, past conduct, history relating to drug or alcohol abuse, criminal history, and record concerning appearance at court proceedings; and
   (B) whether, at the time of the current offense or arrest, the person was on probation, on parole, or on other release pending trial, sentencing, appeal, or completion of sentence for an offense under Federal, State, or local law; and
(4) the nature and seriousness of the danger to any person or the community that would be posed by the person's release.[32]

---

30. *Id.* at 747 n.4. The Court also rejected the claim that the Act violates the prohibition against excessive bail.
31. *See* S. Rep. No. 98-225, at 23 (1983), *reprinted in* 1984 U.S.C.C.A.N. 3182, 3206.
32. 18 U.S.C. § 3142(g).

The Seventh Circuit has warned that the trial court may not disregard any of these factors.[33] The Ninth Circuit has said that, of the four factors, the weight of the evidence against the defendant is least important.[34]

Several courts have held that the probable length of pretrial detention is not a proper consideration in the judicial officer's determination of whether to release the defendant, because it has no bearing on the two concerns addressed by the Act: likelihood to flee and dangerousness.[35] The Second Circuit found error where the district court relied primarily on the demeanor of the defendant, since demeanor is not one of the factors listed in the statute.[36] The First Circuit held that the court may consider prior arrests as part of criminal history even though the defendant was not convicted on the charges.[37] The D.C. and Third Circuits stated that findings should be based on evidence presented at the detention hearing, not on extraneous information.[38]

---

33. United States v. Torres, 929 F.2d 291 (7th Cir. 1991). The district judge explicitly discounted the defendant's "family ties," a factor listed in section 3142(g)(3)(A) as relevant to likelihood of flight, on the ground that defendant's love for his family "does not increase the likelihood of his appearance because prison, his alternative to flight, also would sever those bonds." *Id.* The Seventh Circuit criticized this approach, stating that "[i]f, as the statute provides, family ties are relevant to the probability of flight, a judge may not rebuff all evidence about the subject." *Id.* at 292.

34. United States v. Gebro, 948 F.2d 1118, 1121 (9th Cir. 1991); United States v. Winsor, 785 F.2d 755, 757 (9th Cir. 1986); United States v. Motamedi, 767 F.2d 1403, 1408 (9th Cir. 1985).

35. United States v. Quartermaine, 913 F.2d 910, 917 (11th Cir. 1990); United States v. Hare, 873 F.2d 796, 799 (5th Cir. 1989); United States v. Colombo, 777 F.2d 96, 100 (2d Cir. 1985). However, where detention has in fact been prolonged, reconsideration of the detention order may be required. *See infra* Part IV.B.

36. United States v. Shakur, 817 F.2d 189, 200 (2d Cir.) ("[An] assessment of demeanor often may be a helpful aid to the court.... [H]owever, where the factors enunciated by Congress compel the conclusion that the defendant should be detained, the court may not second guess Congress by relying almost exclusively on an extrastatutory inquiry."), *cert. denied,* 484 U.S. 840 (1987).

37. United States v. Acevedo-Ramos, 755 F.2d 203, 209 (1st Cir. 1985).

38. United States v. Vortis, 785 F.2d 327, 329 (D.C. Cir.) (per curiam) (determination of likely flight should not be based on previous pretrial proceedings), *cert. denied,* 479 U.S. 841 (1986); United States v. Accetturo, 783 F.2d 382, 392 (3d Cir. 1986) (determination should not be based on evidence produced at codefendant's hearing).

D. Standard of Proof

The statute specifies that a finding that no conditions will reasonably ensure the safety of any other person or the community must be supported by clear and convincing evidence.[39] It fails to specify the standard of proof for a finding that no conditions will reasonably ensure the defendant's appearance. The courts have held that such a finding must be supported only by a preponderance of the evidence.[40]

E. Definition of Dangerousness

Defendants may be detained because of the risk of danger to the community even where there is no showing that they are likely to engage in physical violence. The legislative history of the statute indicates that Congress regards drug trafficking as a danger to the community.[41] The Ninth Circuit recognizes economic danger to the community as requiring detention.[42]

The Third Circuit interprets the statute as authorizing pretrial detention based on danger to the community only upon a finding that the defendant is likely to commit one of the offenses specified in

---

39. 18 U.S.C. § 3142(f).

40. United States v. Patriarca, 948 F.2d 789, 793 (1st Cir. 1991); United States v. Aitken, 898 F.2d 104, 107 (9th Cir. 1990); United States v. King, 849 F.2d 485, 489 (11th Cir. 1988); United States v. McConnell, 842 F.2d 105, 110 (5th Cir. 1988) (en banc); United States v. Jackson, 823 F.2d 4, 5 (2d Cir. 1987); United States v. Vortis, 785 F.2d 327, 328–29 (D.C. Cir.) (per curiam), *cert. denied,* 479 U.S. 841 (1986); United States v. Portes, 786 F.2d 758, 765 (7th Cir. 1985); United States v. Orta, 760 F.2d 887, 891 n.20 (8th Cir. 1985). *See also* United States v. Xulam, 84 F.3d 441, 443 (D.C. Cir. 1996) (per curiam) (revoking order of detention because government failed to sustain burden that there was no condition or combination of conditions that would reasonably ensure the presence of the defendant at future proceedings). The courts have reasoned that, in light of Congress's specification that a finding of dangerousness requires a high level of proof, its silence regarding risk of flight suggests that it did not intend to require a high level of proof for risk of flight.

41. S. Rep. No. 98-225, at 12–13 (1983), *reprinted in* 1984 U.S.C.C.A.N. 3182, 3195–96. *See* United States v. Williams, 753 F.2d 329, 335 (4th Cir. 1985) (district court erred in failing to take into account drug dealing as a danger to the community); United States v. Perry, 788 F.2d 100, 113 (3d Cir.), *cert. denied,* 479 U.S. 864 (1986); United States v. Leon, 766 F.2d 77, 81 (2d Cir. 1985).

42. United States v. Reynolds, 956 F.2d 192 (9th Cir. 1992) (defendant convicted of mail fraud under 18 U.S.C. § 1341 (frauds and swindles) posed an economic or pecuniary danger to the community).

section 3142(f).[43] The Second Circuit appears to agree,[44] although it seems to reject the contention that evidence of dangerousness must involve the likelihood of conduct related to the offense the defendant is charged with.[45]

F. Detention Hearing

1. Statutory Requirements

Section 3142(f)(1) provides that a detention hearing shall be held on the government's motion[46] in a case involving (1) a crime of violence; (2) an offense carrying a penalty of life imprisonment or death; (3) a federal drug offense carrying a penalty of ten years or more; or (4) any felony following convictions for two or more of the above three offenses, two or more comparable state or local offenses, or a combination of such offenses. The court may hold a hearing on its own motion or the government's motion in a case that involves serious risk of flight or serious risk that the person will attempt to obstruct justice.[47]

Although some courts have detained defendants in circumstances other than those listed in section 3142(f), the First, Third, and Fifth Circuits, the only circuits to address the question directly, held that defendants may not be detained unless they fit into one of the four categories described above.[48] However, the Fifth Circuit made clear

---

43. United States v. Himler, 797 F.2d 156, 160 (3d Cir. 1986) (likelihood that defendant would commit another crime involving false identification was insufficient basis for pretrial detention). The grounds specified in section 3142 are discussed in Part II.F.

44. United States v. Friedman, 837 F.2d 48, 49 (2d Cir. 1988).

45. United States v. Rodriguez, 950 F.2d 85, 88 (2d Cir. 1991) (district court erred in holding that evidence of defendant's violence was irrelevant because it was unconnected to his charged drug offense). The court cited for support *United States v. Quartermaine*, 913 F.2d 910, 917 (11th Cir. 1990), where defendant was charged with drug possession, yet the Eleventh Circuit considered his unrelated acts of domestic violence evidence of dangerousness (albeit without discussing the fact that the acts were unrelated to the charged crime).

46. The motion need not be in writing. United States v. Volksen, 766 F.2d 190, 192 (5th Cir. 1985).

47. 18 U.S.C. § 3142(f)(2).

48. United States v. Byrd, 969 F.2d 106, 110 (5th Cir. 1992) (detention order vacated because government did not establish that to knowingly receive child pornography through the mail was covered by section 3142(f)); United States v. Ploof, 851 F.2d 7, 11 (1st Cir. 1988) (evidence of defendant's plans to kill someone did not justify detention when charged offenses

that section 3142(f) applies if the case against the defendant "involves" a crime of violence, that is, if the offense with which the defendant was charged is "reasonably connected" to acts of violence, even if the offense is not itself a crime of violence.[49]

A "crime of violence" is

(A) an offense that has as an element of the offense the use, attempted use, or threatened use of physical force against the person or property of another; [or]
(B) any other offense that is a felony and that, by its nature, involves a substantial risk that physical force against the person or property of another may be used in the course of committing the offense.[50]

The Second Circuit has held that conspiracy to commit armed robbery is a crime of violence under section 3142(f).[51] That circuit has also held that a defendant charged with a RICO conspiracy can be considered to be charged with a crime of violence under this section even if he is not

---

involved white-collar crimes not covered by section 3142(f); case remanded to see if the person whom defendant allegedly intended to harm was a witness, in which case detention would be proper pursuant to section 3142(f)(2)(B)'s obstruction of justice provision); United States v. Friedman, 837 F.2d 48, 49 (2d Cir. 1988) (detention order vacated because district court finding regarding risk of flight was clearly erroneous and the defendant had not been charged with any of the crimes enumerated in section 3142(f)(1)); United States v. Himler, 797 F.2d 156, 160 (3d Cir. 1986) (defendant charged with false identification could not be detained absent proof of risk of flight). As noted *supra* note 45 and accompanying text, *United States v. Rodriguez*, 950 F.2d 85, 88 (2d Cir. 1991), and *United States v. Quartermaine*, 913 F.2d 910, 917 (11th Cir. 1990), suggest that there need not be a nexus between the charged offense and the evidence of dangerousness. This is not inconsistent with the First, Third, and Fifth Circuits' holdings that defendants may be detained only if one of the circumstances listed in section 3142(f) is present. In *Rodriguez* and *Quartermaine*, defendants *were* charged with offenses listed in section 3142(f). Thus, the two lines of cases may be reconciled as follows: a detention hearing is authorized only if it involves one of the circumstances listed in section 3142(f), but when such a circumstance is present, dangers posed by the defendant unrelated to that circumstance may be considered by the judicial officer pursuant to section 3142(g)(4), which permits consideration generally of danger to any person or the community.

49. *Byrd*, 969 F.2d at 110. The government adduced evidence that defendant, charged with knowingly receiving child pornography through the mail, was a danger to the community because he was a child molester. The Fifth Circuit held, however, that because the government did not establish that the charged crime "involve[d]" an act of violence, defendant could not be detained.

50. 18 U.S.C. § 3156(a)(4).

51. United States v. Chimurenga, 760 F.2d 400, 403–04 (2d Cir. 1985).

named in the indictment in a predicate act that constitutes a crime of violence.[52]

The circuits are split on the question of whether a violation of 18 U.S.C. § 922(g)(1), which prohibits possession of a firearm by a felon, constitutes a crime of violence within the meaning of section 3156(a)(4). The Second and Tenth hold that it does.[53] The Third, Seventh, Eleventh, and D.C. Circuits hold that a felon-in-possession charge does not meet the definition of section 3156(a)(4).[54]

The determination of whether firearm offenses or other types of offenses meet the definition of a "crime of violence" in section 3156(a)(4) is based on an examination of the nature of the charged offense and not the specific facts and circumstances of the offense. In other words, the proper analytical approach is a "categorical" rather than a "case-by-case" approach.[55]

2. Timing of Detention Motion and Hearing

a. Statutory requirement; remedy for a violation

A detention hearing must be held immediately upon the defendant's first appearance before a judicial officer unless the defendant or the government seeks a continuance.[56] Generally, "first appearance" means just that.[57] However, the Eighth Circuit suggested that this requirement is not violated when a detention hearing is held upon discovery of new evidence relevant to the likelihood of flight or obstruction of justice

---

52. United States v. Ciccone, 312 F.3d 535, 541 (2d Cir. 2002).
53. United States v. Dillard, 214 F.3d 88 (2d Cir. 2000), *cert. denied,* 532 U.S. 907 (2001); United States v. Rogers, 371 F.3d 1225 (10th Cir. 2004). The Tenth Circuit also held that possession of a firearm by a person convicted of a misdemeanor domestic violence offense is, contrary to 18 U.S.C. § 922(g)(9), a crime of violence for purposes of the Bail Reform Act. *Rogers,* 371 F.3d at 1232.
54. United States v. Bowers, 432 F.3d 518 (3d Cir. 2005); United States v. Johnson, 399 F.3d 1297, 1298 (11th Cir. 2005); United States v. Lane, 252 F.3d 905 (7th Cir. 2001); United States v. Singleton, 182 F.3d 7, 12 (D.C. Cir. 1999).
55. *Bowers,* 432 F.3d at 520–21; *Rogers,* 371 F.3d at 1229 n.5; *Singleton,* 182 F.3d at 10–12.
56. 18 U.S.C. § 3142(f).
57. *See, e.g.,* United States v. Payden, 759 F.2d 202, 204–05 (2d Cir. 1985) (construing statute strictly).

even if the defendant has already appeared before a judicial officer.[58] The Fifth Circuit disagreed.[59] The Third and Eighth Circuits have held that the first-appearance requirement is not violated when a detention hearing is held at the defendant's first appearance before the district judge even if the defendant has already appeared before a magistrate judge who did not hold a hearing.[60] A hearing may be reopened, either before or after a determination by the judicial officer, if the movant proffers material evidence that was previously unavailable.[61]

In *United States v. Montalvo-Murillo*,[62] the Supreme Court held that the failure to comply with the time requirements of section 3142(f) need not result in a defendant's release.[63] The defendant had made several court appearances at proceedings that were not detention hearings. Eventually, a magistrate judge held a detention hearing and, finding that the defendant was neither a flight risk nor dangerous, ordered him released. On review of the order, the district court found that the defendant did, in fact, pose a danger to the community, but nevertheless ordered the defendant released because of noncompliance with section 3142(f)'s time requirements.[64] The Tenth Circuit affirmed.[65]

The Supreme Court reversed: "Neither the timing requirements nor any other part of the Act can be read to require, or even suggest, that a timing error must result in release of a person who should otherwise be detained."[66] Thus, "once the Government discovers that the

---

58. United States v. Holloway, 781 F.2d 124, 126 (8th Cir. 1984).

59. United States v. O'Shaughnessy, 764 F.2d 1035, 1037–39 (5th Cir.), *vacated on reh'g as moot*, 772 F.2d 112 (5th Cir. 1985). *Cf.* United States v. Fortna, 769 F.2d 243, 248–49 (5th Cir. 1985) (any error was harmless where magistrate judge ordered detention hearing held five days after defendant first appeared and expressed a desire to hire counsel).

60. United States v. Maull, 773 F.2d 1479, 1482–85 (8th Cir. 1985) (en banc); United States v. Delker, 757 F.2d 1390, 1394 (3d Cir. 1985).

61. 18 U.S.C. § 3142(f).

62. 495 U.S. 711 (1990).

63. Prior to *Montalvo-Murillo*, untimely detention hearings had resulted in release in several cases. *See, e.g.*, United States v. Molinaro, 876 F.2d 1432, 1433 (9th Cir. 1989) (per curiam); United States v. Al-Azzawy, 768 F.2d 1141, 1145–46 (9th Cir. 1985); United States v. Payden, 759 F.2d 202, 203 (2d Cir. 1985); *O'Shaughnessy*, 764 F.2d at 1036–37.

64. United States v. Montalvo-Murillo, 713 F. Supp. 1407 (D.N.M. 1989).

65. United States v. Montalvo-Murillo, 876 F.2d 826 (10th Cir. 1989).

66. United States v. Montalvo-Murillo, 495 U.S. 711, 716–17 (1990).

time limits have expired, it may ask for a prompt detention hearing."[67] The Court implied that such a hearing should be granted and that the timing error should ordinarily not result in release, but acknowledged that "[i]t is conceivable that some combination of procedural irregularities could render a detention hearing so flawed that it would not constitute 'a hearing pursuant to [section 3142] subsection (f).'"[68] The Court also left open the possibility of some remedy—other than release of the defendant—for a violation of the timing requirements of section 3142(f).[69] Thus, the Court made clear that, although a violation of section 3142(f) need not result in release, the timing requirements are nevertheless binding on the judicial officer.[70]

Courts have interpreted the requirement flexibly in one common circumstance, holding that where the defendant is arrested outside the charging district, the detention hearing may be held at the first appearance following removal.[71]

b. Continuances

The detention hearing must be held immediately, unless the defendant or the government moves for a continuance. The statute sharply limits the length of continuances. Except for good cause, continuances are limited to three days for the government and five days for the defendant.[72] The Ninth and Eleventh Circuits have said that convenience of counsel or the court does not satisfy the good-cause requirement.[73] The Eleventh Circuit held that a magistrate judge erred in granting a continuance of more than five days to permit other defendants to ob-

---

67. *Id.* at 721.
68. *Id.* at 717.
69. *Id.* at 721 ("Whatever other remedies may exist for detention without a timely hearing [is] . . . a matter not before us here.").
70. *Id.*
71. United States v. Valenzuela-Verdigo, 815 F.2d 1011, 1016 (5th Cir. 1987); United States v. Melendez-Carrion, 790 F.2d 984, 990 (2d Cir. 1986); United States v. Dominguez, 783 F.2d 702, 704–05 (7th Cir. 1986).
72. 18 U.S.C. § 3142(f). This section was amended in 1996 to resolve a split in the circuits, and to clarify that the five- and three-day limitations on the length of continuances of detention hearings do not include intermediate Saturdays, Sundays, and legal holidays.
73. United States v. Al-Azzawy, 768 F.2d 1141, 1146 (9th Cir. 1985); United States v. Hurtado, 779 F.2d 1467, 1476 (11th Cir. 1985).

tain counsel.[74] The Second Circuit held the good-cause requirement to be satisfied by "substantial reasons pertinent to protection of the rights of the defendants"[75]—the need to obtain witnesses and affidavits from abroad and the need for defense counsel to obtain interpreters to help interview non–English-speaking clients.

The First and Fifth Circuits deem defendants to have acquiesced in a continuance if they do not make a timely objection to a proposed continuance.[76]

The statute provides for a continuance on motion of defense counsel or the government, but makes no explicit provision for a continuance on the court's own motion. The Ninth and Eleventh Circuits have held that detention hearings may not be continued on the court's own motion.[77] The D.C. and Fifth Circuits have permitted such continuances in special circumstances.[78] During a continuance, the defendant shall be detained. Further, on its own motion or the government's, the court may order a medical examination of a person who appears to be a narcotics addict to determine whether he or she is one.

---

74. *Hurtado*, 779 F.2d at 1474 n.7 (eight-day delay).
75. United States v. Melendez-Carrion, 790 F.2d 984, 991–92 (2d Cir. 1986).
76. United States v. Araneda, 899 F.2d 368, 370 (5th Cir. 1990) (it was error for court to grant continuance for all codefendants when only some requested it; court of appeals nevertheless affirmed because counsel were advised of the continuance and did not object); United States v. King, 818 F.2d 112, 115 n.3 (1st Cir. 1987) (failure to hold formal detention hearing prior to initial detention order not reversible error where defendant did not request such a hearing and was in state custody). *See also* United States v. Madruga, 810 F.2d 1010, 1014 (11th Cir. 1987) ("Unless a defendant objects to the proposed hearing date on the stated ground that the assigned date exceeds the three-day maximum, he is deemed to acquiesce in up to a five-day continuance."); United States v. Coonan, 826 F.2d 1180, 1184 (2d Cir. 1987) (defense counsel told the government that "bail was not an issue," thereby implicitly waiving defendant's right to a hearing within five days).
77. United States v. Al-Azzawy, 768 F.2d 1141, 1146 (9th Cir. 1985); *Hurtado*, 779 F.2d at 1475–76.
78. United States v. Alatishe, 768 F.2d 364, 369 (D.C. Cir. 1985) (seven-day continuance on motion of the court upheld; delay caused in part by confusion over requirements of the new statute, and neither party objected to continuance; court of appeals noted that "in future cases, except in the most compelling situations, the judicial officer should not act *sua sponte* to delay the detention hearing"). *See also* United States v. Fortna, 769 F.2d 243, 249 (5th Cir. 1985) (magistrate judge permitted to set detention hearing for five days later to enable defendant to obtain counsel).

c. Waiver by defendant

The only circuits to consider the question have held that defendants may waive the right to a detention hearing (or a hearing within the statutorily prescribed time frame). In a Fourth Circuit case, the defendants told the magistrate judge that they wanted to remain in custody for their own protection. As a result, the magistrate judge did not conduct an evidentiary hearing or make written findings. Later, however, the defendants moved for their immediate release on the ground that they had an unwaivable right to a detention hearing. The original panel agreed, but the en banc court held that defendants may waive both the time requirements and the detention hearing itself.[79] The Second Circuit reached the same conclusion.[80]

The timing provisions present special problems when a defendant is in state custody at the time that the detention hearing should be held. Any determination of release or detention in the federal case is moot if the defendant will be returned to custody in the other jurisdiction. If the defendant's status in the other jurisdiction changes, however, a detention hearing becomes meaningful. The First Circuit has suggested that in these situations the judge should either hold a provisional detention hearing, which would be effective upon any change in status, or postpone the detention hearing if the government and the defendant agree. If the defendant objects to any postponement of the hearing, the judge should assess whether the hearing should be continued for good cause pursuant to section 3142(f).[81] It should be noted that the Interstate Agreement on Detainers Act may be implicated upon the transfer of a defendant in custody from one jurisdiction to another.[82]

---

79. United States v. Clark, 865 F.2d 1433, 1436 (4th Cir. 1989) (en banc).

80. United States v. Coonan, 826 F.2d 1180, 1184 (2d Cir. 1987) (to hold that hearing or time limit cannot be waived "would convert the time requirements of the act into a potential trap, available to defendants, that would undermine the functioning of the act, and would also require meaningless, ritualistic hearings in situations where no one wants them").

81. United States v. King, 818 F.2d 112, 115 n.3 (1st Cir. 1987). *See also Coonan*, 826 F.2d at 1185.

82. 18 U.S.C. App. 2.

G. Rebuttable Presumptions

1. The Two Presumptions

The statute creates two rebuttable presumptions: the "previous-violator presumption" and the "drug-and-firearm-offender presumption." The previous-violator presumption is that no conditions of release will reasonably ensure the safety of the community where the defendant is accused of one of numerous specified crimes, such as crimes of violence, and has previously been convicted of committing one of the specified crimes while free on bail.

The drug-and-firearm-offender presumption is that no conditions of release will reasonably ensure the defendant's appearance and the safety of the community where a judicial officer finds probable cause to believe that the defendant has committed certain enumerated offenses. The provision is often referred to as the drug-and-firearm-offender provision because it originally included only federal drug offenses carrying a maximum prison term of ten years or more and offenses in which the defendant is alleged to have used a firearm to commit the offense. Congress has since added, however, certain terrorism-related offenses and certain sex offenses involving minor victims.[83]

As of this writing, no published case law specifically addresses the previous-violator presumption. However, the First Circuit has suggested that an analysis of the drug-and-firearm-offender presumption, discussed below, would also apply to the previous-violator presumption.[84]

2. Application of "Drug-and-Firearm-Offender Presumption"

a. Ten-year maximum charge required

The Eleventh Circuit held that for drug charges to trigger the drug-and-firearm-offender presumption, the defendant must be charged with at least one offense separately carrying a ten-year (or longer) maximum

---

83. 18 U.S.C. § 3142(e).
84. United States v. Jessup, 757 F.2d 378, 381 (1st Cir. 1985).

sentence. The presumption does not arise simply because the combined maximum sentences on all drug charges exceed ten years.[85]

The First and Fifth Circuits held that the presumption applies whenever the offense carries a penalty of ten years or more, even if the defendant is unlikely to receive a ten-year sentence under the Sentencing Guidelines.[86] However, the sentence that the defendant is likely to receive can affect the weight given to the presumption.[87]

b. Probable cause and grand jury indictments

Most courts have held that where a grand jury has indicted a defendant on one of the predicate offenses, a judicial officer need not make an independent finding of probable cause to invoke the drug-and-firearm-offender presumption.[88] Rather, the indictment itself establishes probable cause that the defendant committed the offense and triggers the presumption that the defendant poses a danger to the community and is a flight risk.

c. Formal charge required

The Second Circuit held that the drug-and-firearm-offender presumption cannot arise if the defendant has not yet been charged with the firearm offense by a "valid complaint or indictment," even if there may be probable cause to believe that the defendant appearing at a detention hearing on other charges has also committed a firearm violation.[89]

---

85. United States v. Hinote, 789 F.2d 1490, 1491 (11th Cir. 1986).
86. United States v. Carr, 947 F.2d 1239, 1240 (5th Cir. 1992) (per curiam); United States v. Moss, 887 F.2d 333, 336–37 (1st Cir. 1989).
87. *Moss*, 887 F.2d at 337.
88. United States v. Stricklin, 932 F.2d 1353, 1355 (10th Cir. 1991); United States v. King, 849 F.2d 485, 488 (11th Cir. 1988); United States v. Jackson, 845 F.2d 1262, 1265 (5th Cir. 1988); United States v. Vargas, 804 F.2d 157, 161 (1st Cir. 1986); United States v. Suppa, 799 F.2d 115, 118–19 (3d Cir. 1986); United States v. Dominguez, 783 F.2d 702, 706 n.7 (7th Cir. 1986); United States v. Contreras, 776 F.2d 51, 54–55 (2d Cir. 1985); United States v. Hazime, 762 F.2d 34, 37 (6th Cir. 1985); United States v. Hurtado, 779 F.2d 1467, 1477–79 (11th Cir. 1985).
89. United States v. Chimurenga, 760 F.2d 400, 405 (2d Cir. 1985).

d. Effect of presumption

The drug-and-firearm-offender presumption imposes on defendants only a burden of production; the burden of persuasion concerning the risk of flight and dangerousness remains with the government.[90] However, courts have held that when a defendant comes forward with no evidence, the presumption alone supports the conclusion that no conditions of release could reasonably ensure the appearance of the defendant and the safety of the community.[91]

To meet its burden, the defense must produce only "some [relevant] evidence."[92] The introduction of such evidence, however, does not eliminate the presumption entirely.[93] Rather, the presumption "remains in the case as one of the elements to be considered" by the judicial officer.[94] This ensures that the court takes note of the congressional findings that drug traffickers pose special flight risks.[95]

The Seventh Circuit held that to rebut the presumption, defendants need not produce evidence that they are innocent of the charged crime.[96] Rather, they may show that "the specific nature of the crimes

---

90. United States v. Moss, 887 F.2d 333, 338 (1st Cir. 1989); United States v. Hare, 873 F.2d 796, 798 (5th Cir. 1989); United States v. Martir, 782 F.2d 1141, 1144 (2d Cir. 1986); United States v. Perry, 788 F.2d 100, 115 (3d Cir.), *cert. denied,* 479 U.S. 864 (1986); United States v. Dominguez, 783 F.2d 702, 707 (7th Cir. 1986); United States v. Portes, 786 F.2d 758, 764 (7th Cir. 1985); United States v. Alatishe, 768 F.2d 364, 371 n.14 (D.C. Cir. 1985); United States v. Jessup, 757 F.2d 378, 381–84, 389 (1st Cir. 1985); *Chimurenga,* 760 F.2d at 405; United States v. Fortna, 769 F.2d 243, 253 n.11 (5th Cir. 1985); United States v. Diaz, 777 F.2d 1236, 1237 (7th Cir. 1985); United States v. Hurtado, 779 F.2d 1467, 1470 n.4 (11th Cir. 1985); United States v. Orta, 760 F.2d 887, 891 n.17 (8th Cir. 1985).

91. *Perry,* 788 F.2d at 107; *Alatishe,* 768 F.2d at 371; United States v. Daniels, 772 F.2d 382, 383 (7th Cir. 1985).

92. *Jessup,* 757 F.2d at 381.

93. United States v. Dillon, 938 F.2d 1412, 1416 (1st Cir. 1991) ("rebutted presumption retains evidentiary weight"); *Hare,* 873 F.2d at 798 ("presumption is not a mere 'bursting bubble' that totally disappears from the judge's consideration after the defendant comes forward with evidence"); *Dominguez,* 783 F.2d at 707; *Martir,* 782 F.2d at 1144.

94. Montgomery County Fire Bd. v. Fisher, 454 A.2d 394, 400 (1983), *quoted with approval in Jessup,* 757 F.2d at 383.

95. The First Circuit has stated that the remaining weight of the presumption "depend[s] on how closely defendant's case resembles the congressional paradigm." United States v. Palmer-Contreras, 835 F.2d 15, 18 (1st Cir. 1987).

96. United States v. Dominguez, 783 F.2d 702, 707 (7th Cir. 1986). *But cf.* United States v. Rueben, 974 F.2d 580, 587 (5th Cir. 1992), *cert. denied,* 507 U.S. 940 (1993) (presumption unrebutted because defendants presented no evidence that they would not continue to engage

charged, or . . . something about their individual circumstances" suggests that they are not dangerous or likely to flee.[97]

The Fifth Circuit held that circumstances are relevant only if germane to the likelihood of flight or a presumption of dangerousness; it therefore dismissed as irrelevant a defendant's contention that detention imposed a severe financial hardship.[98]

The Fifth Circuit stated that, where there has been a full evidentiary hearing in which both sides have presented evidence, "the shifting of and the descriptions of evidentiary burdens become largely irrelevant and the question becomes whether the evidence as a whole supports the conclusions" reached by the trial court.[99]

e. Constitutionality

The First Circuit held that the presumption, when construed not to shift the burden of persuasion, does not violate the Due Process Clause of the Fifth Amendment.[100] The Third Circuit held that because the presumption of dangerousness may place the defendant in the position of risking self-incrimination or submitting to pretrial detention, the judicial officer should grant use immunity to a defendant who seeks to rebut the presumption through his or her own testimony.[101] In an unpublished opinion, the Sixth Circuit appeared to reject this approach.[102] In a case where the presumption did not apply, the Fifth

---

in drug trafficking if released on bail); United States v. Hare, 873 F.2d 796, 799 (5th Cir. 1989) (same).

97. *Dominguez*, 783 F.2d at 707. Defendants must rebut the presumption of both dangerousness and likelihood of flight. United States v. Daniels, 772 F.2d 382, 383 (7th Cir. 1985) (assuming defendant showed he was unlikely to flee, he could still be detained on unrebutted presumption of dangerousness). *Cf.* United States v. Carbone, 793 F.2d 559, 561 (3d Cir. 1986) (per curiam) (under the circumstances, evidence normally adduced to rebut presumption of flight also rebutted presumption of dangerousness).

98. Fassler v. United States, 858 F.2d 1016, 1018 n.5 (5th Cir. 1988) (per curiam), *cert. denied*, 490 U.S. 1099 (1989).

99. United States v. Trosper, 809 F.2d 1107, 1111 (5th Cir. 1987).

100. United States v. Jessup, 757 F.2d 378, 384–87 (1st Cir. 1985).

101. United States v. Perry, 788 F.2d 100, 115–16 (3d Cir.), *cert. denied*, 479 U.S. 864 (1986).

102. United States v. Dean, 927 F.2d 605 (6th Cir.) (table), *cert. denied*, 502 U.S. 838 (1991) (rejecting claim that use of defendant's testimony at detention hearing in subsequent trial violated his right against self-incrimination).

Circuit rejected a facial challenge to the statute based on its alleged violation of the self-incrimination clause.[103] The Second Circuit held that it is not error to prohibit the government from cross-examining the detainee in order to prevent self-incrimination problems.[104]

H. Temporary Detention

Section 3142(d) authorizes a judicial officer to order an arrestee temporarily detained for up to ten days if the person is arrested while on pretrial or post-trial release, probation, or parole, or is an alien not admitted to permanent residence, and the judicial officer finds that the arrestee "may flee or pose a danger to any other person or the community."[105] The court must direct the government to notify the appropriate authorities so that they can take the person into custody. If these authorities do not take the defendant into custody within the ten-day period, a section 3142(f) hearing may be held on the more recent offense. This hearing is separate from the section 3142(d) hearing, and the judicial officer cannot rely on facts previously found to support a section 3142(d) detention.[106]

All the courts that have considered the question have interpreted section 3142(d) as permitting the government to move under section 3142(f) for a detention hearing at any time during the ten-day period, rather than at the defendant's first appearance as normally required by section 3142(f).[107] (However, the Fifth and D.C. Circuits have indicated that the better practice is for the government to move under both section 3142(d) and section 3142(f) at the defendant's initial appear-

---

103. United States v. Parker, 848 F.2d 61, 62 (5th Cir. 1988) (per curiam), *cert. denied,* 493 U.S. 871 (1989). The court left open the possibility that use immunity might be required where the rebuttable presumption applies. *Id.* at n.1. *See also* United States v. Ingraham, 832 F.2d 229, 237–38 (1st Cir. 1987) (rejecting the claim that use immunity should be granted in a case where the presumption did not apply; leaving open the possibility that it is required when the presumption applies), *cert. denied,* 486 U.S. 1009 (1988).

104. United States v. Shakur, 817 F.2d 189, 200 (2d Cir.), *cert. denied,* 484 U.S. 840 (1987).

105. 18 U.S.C. § 3142(d)(2).

106. United States v. Alatishe, 768 F.2d 364, 370 (D.C. Cir. 1985).

107. United States v. Moncada-Pelaez, 810 F.2d 1008, 1010 (11th Cir. 1987); United States v. Vargas, 804 F.2d 157, 161 (1st Cir. 1986); United States v. Becerra-Cobo, 790 F.2d 427, 430 (5th Cir. 1986); United States v. Lee, 783 F.2d 92, 94 (7th Cir. 1986); *Alatishe,* 768 F.2d at 368.

ance.[108]) The Fifth, D.C., and Ninth Circuits have indicated that continuances under section 3142(f) cannot extend the detention period beyond ten days.[109] The Seventh Circuit held otherwise.[110]

The First Circuit has emphasized that it is important for the judicial officer to make clear under which provision detention is being considered. In *United States v. Vargas*,[111] defendants, already detained under section 3142(d), appeared before a magistrate judge for arraignment on another offense. The government indicated that it would "seek to detain" the defendants. The magistrate judge, apparently believing that defense counsel had waived argument on the detention issue, ordered the defendants detained. One of the defendants subsequently moved for release upon expiration of the ten-day period under section 3142(d), arguing that no timely motion for detention under section 3142(f) had been made. Although it upheld the magistrate judge's detention order,[112] the First Circuit suggested that in order to avoid the type of confusion that led to the appeal, it is important that magistrate judges and district judges closely adhere to the requirements of sections 3142(e) and 3142(f) and to clearly state that they are proceeding under those sections when they are in situations involving the possibility of pretrial detention under section 3142(e).[113]

I. Detention Upon Review of a Release Order

Section 3145(a) permits either the government or the defendant to seek review of release conditions imposed by a magistrate judge or by a judicial officer other than the district court with original jurisdiction or an appellate court. Several circuits interpret this subsection as author-

---

108. *Becerra-Cobo*, 790 F.2d at 430; *Alatishe*, 768 F.2d at 368.
109. *Becerra-Cobo*, 790 F.2d at 430; *Alatishe*, 768 F.2d at 368; United States v. Al-Azzawy, 768 F.2d 1141, 1146 (9th Cir. 1985).
110. *Lee*, 783 F.2d at 94.
111. 804 F.2d 157, 162 (1st Cir. 1986).
112. The court of appeals noted that the magistrate judge had offered the defendants an opportunity for additional, individual hearings; that the magistrate judge held a second hearing six days later, immediately upon expiration of the section 3142(d) detention period; and that the district judge also held a de novo hearing upon review of the magistrate judge's detention order. *Id.* at 160–62.
113. *Id.* at 162.

izing a trial court to impose detention at the time of such review.[114] The Eighth and Ninth Circuits have gone further, holding that district judges can review a magistrate judge's detention order sua sponte and impose detention at that time.[115]

J. Evidence and Right to Counsel

1. Right to Counsel

At the detention hearing, defendants have the right to an attorney and the right to appointed counsel if they cannot afford one.[116] The rules governing admissibility and presentation of evidence in criminal trials do not apply at the detention hearing, and the court has broad discretion to limit the presentation of evidence.[117]

2. Hearsay Evidence

Hearsay evidence is generally admissible at a detention hearing.[118] However, trial courts "should be sensitive to the fact that Congress' authorization of hearsay evidence does not represent a determination that such evidence is always appropriate."[119] The First and Third Circuits advise courts to assess the reliability of hearsay evidence and require corroboration when necessary.[120]

---

114. United States v. Delker, 757 F.2d 1390, 1393–95 (3d Cir. 1985), United States v. Medina, 775 F.2d 1398, 1400–02 (11th Cir. 1985). These courts observed that section 3145(a) authorizes the district judge to conduct de novo review of a magistrate judge's release order, and reasoned that the district judge should therefore have open all the options available to the magistrate judge.

115. United States v. Gebro, 948 F.2d 1118, 1120 (9th Cir. 1991); United States v. Maull, 773 F.2d 1479, 1486 (8th Cir. 1985) (en banc).

116. 18 U.S.C. § 3142(f).

117. *Id.*

118. United States v. Cardenas, 784 F.2d 937, 938 (9th Cir.) (per curiam), *vacated as moot*, 792 F.2d 906 (9th Cir. 1986); United States v. Acevedo-Ramos, 755 F.2d 203, 208 (1st Cir. 1985); United States v. Delker, 757 F.2d 1390, 1397 (3d Cir. 1985); United States v. Fortna, 769 F.2d 243, 250 (5th Cir. 1985).

119. United States v. Accetturo, 783 F.2d 382, 389 (3d Cir. 1986).

120. *Id.*; *Acevedo-Ramos*, 755 F.2d at 207–08.

3. Proffer Evidence

Section 3142(f) states that defendants may "present information by proffer or otherwise." The Third Circuit held that the judicial officer may require the defendant to proffer evidence rather than to present live testimony.[121] The Seventh Circuit held to the contrary.[122] Several circuits have held that the government may also proceed by way of proffer.[123] The Third Circuit, however, questioned the validity of relying on a proffer by the government to establish probable cause that the accused committed one of the offenses giving rise to the drug-and-firearm-offender presumption under section 3142(e).[124]

4. Cross-Examination

Section 3142(f) affords defendants an opportunity to cross-examine witnesses appearing at the hearing, but it makes no explicit provision for nonappearing witnesses. Several courts have held that, at least where the defendant makes no specific proffer of how cross-examination will counter the government's proffered evidence, the court is not required to subpoena the government witnesses.[125] The Third Circuit noted a few circumstances that militate in favor of subpoenaing a requested witness: the defendant's offer of specific evidence showing unreliability, the lack of a need to protect confidentiality, and

---

121. *Delker,* 757 F.2d at 1395–96.
122. United States v. Torres, 929 F.2d 291, 292 (7th Cir. 1991).
123. United States v. Gaviria, 828 F.2d 667, 669 (11th Cir. 1987); United States v. Martir, 782 F.2d 1141, 1147 (2d Cir. 1986); United States v. Cardenas, 784 F.2d 937, 938 (9th Cir.) (per curiam), *vacated as moot,* 792 F.2d 906 (9th Cir. 1986).
124. United States v. Suppa, 799 F.2d 115, 118 (3d Cir. 1986).
125. United States v. Accetturo, 783 F.2d 382, 388 (3d Cir. 1986) (there was no error in failing to compel appearance of government witness for cross-examination where there was no reason to believe witness would have testified favorably to defendants); United States v. Winsor, 785 F.2d 755, 756–57 (9th Cir. 1986) (where defendant did not make proffer to show that government's proffer was incorrect, defendant did not have right to cross-examine investigators); *Delker,* 757 F.2d at 1397–98 n.4 (there was no error in declining to subpoena witnesses; the question whether there is a right to cross-examine where defendant makes specific proffer negating government's case was left open). *See also Cardenas,* 784 F.2d at 938 (there was no error in refusing to subpoena witnesses where government withdrew proffered evidence challenged by defendant).

the prospect of lengthy detention.[126] The Eleventh Circuit indicated that if a finding of dangerousness or likelihood of flight rests on the weight of the evidence against the defendant with respect to the charged crime, it would be reversible error not to give the defendant the opportunity to cross-examine witnesses.[127]

5. Ex Parte Evidence

The Bail Reform Act does not specifically address the use of evidence presented ex parte. The Second Circuit, in a post-conviction release hearing, held that the right to a fair hearing implicit in section 3143(a)(1) requires some notice to the defendant of the reasons for detention advanced by the government. Receipt of ex parte evidence should satisfy three criteria: (1) satisfaction of the factors outlined in *Waller v. Georgia*[128] to exclude the public from certain criminal proceedings; (2) disclosure to the defendant of the gist or substance of the government's ex parte submission; and (3) careful scrutiny by the district court of the reliability of the ex parte evidence.[129]

The Third Circuit has held that reliance on ex parte evidence presented is generally inconsistent with the Act's procedural protections.[130] The Third Circuit has also suggested that use of such testimony may run afoul of the confrontation clause.[131] In a brief opinion later vacated

---

126. *Accetturo*, 783 F.2d at 388

127. United States v. Hurtado, 779 F.2d 1467, 1479–80 (11th Cir. 1985) (it was harmless error for district court to quash subpoenas of Drug Enforcement Agency agents where a finding that defendant was likely to flee was based on nature of the offense and history and characteristics of defendants rather than on weight of the evidence).

128. 467 U.S. 39, 48 (1984) (the four factors for closure of a hearing are (1) "the party seeking to close the hearing must advance an overriding interest that is likely to be prejudiced," (2) "the closure must be no broader than necessary to protect that interest," (3) "the trial court must consider reasonable alternatives to closing the proceeding," and (4) "it must make findings adequate to support the closure"). For a case setting forth the factors relevant to restricting public access to pretrial records, including tapes played at the pretrial hearing that were not entered into evidence, see *United States v. Graham*, 257 F.3d 143, 149–56 (2d Cir. 2001).

129. United States v. Abuhamra, 389 F.3d 309, 329 (2d Cir. 2004).

130. *Accetturo*, 783 F.2d at 391 (presentation in camera appropriate only when there is a compelling need and no alternative means of meeting that need).

131. United States v. Perry, 788 F.2d 100, 117 (3d Cir.), *cert. denied*, 479 U.S. 864 (1986).

as moot, the Ninth Circuit rejected a due process challenge to the use of in camera evidence.[132]

6. Challenged Evidence

The First and Eighth Circuits held that a district court may rely on evidence whose legality the accused has challenged, at least until a court rules that the material was not legally obtained.[133]

7. Electronic Surveillance

Both the First and Second Circuits upheld the use of evidence obtained by electronic surveillance.[134] The Second Circuit noted that such material is governed by the ten-day notice requirement of 18 U.S.C. § 2518(9).[135] Acknowledging the potential conflict between the ten-day notice requirement and the requirement of a prompt detention hearing, the Second Circuit pointed out that if prejudice to the defendant would result from waiver of the ten-day notice period, the detention hearing may be continued for good cause under section 3142(f).[136]

8. Psychiatric Examination

The Second Circuit held that judicial officers may not order a psychiatric examination to determine the dangerousness of a defendant; they must base such a determination on evidence adduced at the detention hearing.[137]

---

132. United States v. Cardenas, 784 F.2d 937, 938 (9th Cir.) (per curiam), *vacated as moot*, 792 F.2d 906 (9th Cir. 1986). *See also* United States v. Acevedo-Ramos, 755 F.2d 203, 207–09 (1st Cir. 1985) (magistrate judges may test veracity of hearsay by inspection of evidence in camera where confidentiality of sources is necessary).

133. United States v. Apker, 964 F.2d 742, 744 (8th Cir. 1992) (wiretap challenged); United States v. Angiulo, 755 F.2d 969, 974 (1st Cir. 1985) (electronic surveillance challenged).

134. United States v. Berrios-Berrios, 791 F.2d 246, 253 (2d Cir.), *cert. dismissed*, 479 U.S. 978 (1986); *Angiulo*, 755 F.2d at 974.

135. *Berrios-Berrios*, 791 F.2d at 253.

136. United States v. Salerno, 794 F.2d 64, 70 (2d Cir. 1986), *rev'd on other grounds*, 481 U.S. 739 (1987).

137. United States v. Martin-Trigona, 767 F.2d 35, 38 (2d Cir. 1985).

K. Hearings Involving Multiple Defendants

Cases involving multiple defendants can pose problems. The Eleventh Circuit recommends that the court make individual determinations on continuances rather than automatically schedule all hearings for the same date.[138] The Third Circuit held that evidence offered at hearings of codefendants may not be considered unless the defendant is given a confrontation opportunity at the defendant's own hearing.[139]

Where detention hearings are required for a large number of codefendants, the Second Circuit suggests that the court consider alternatives to individual hearings before the same judicial officer: a joint hearing; consolidation to receive testimony of government witnesses common to all the defendants, followed by individual hearings to receive evidence peculiar to each defendant; and assignment of more than one judicial officer to the hearings.[140]

L. Written Findings

Written findings of fact and a written statement of reasons are required when detention is ordered.[141] The Second Circuit requires that these findings include a statement of the alternatives considered and the reasons for rejecting them.[142]

---

138. United States v. Hurtado, 779 F.2d 1467, 1476 (11th Cir. 1985).
139. United States v. Accetturo, 783 F.2d 382, 392 (3d Cir. 1986).
140. United States v. Melendez-Carrion, 790 F.2d 984, 992–93 (2d Cir. 1986).
141. Fed. R. App. P. 9(a); 18 U.S.C. § 3142(i)(1); United States v. Vortis, 785 F.2d 327, 329 (D.C. Cir.) (per curiam) (remanding for written findings to support detention order), *cert. denied*, 479 U.S. 841 (1986); United States v. Westbrook, 780 F.2d 1185, 1190 (5th Cir. 1986) (same); *Hurtado*, 779 F.2d at 1480–81 (same); United States v. Quinnones, 610 F. Supp. 74, 76 (S.D.N.Y. 1985) (defendant released).
142. United States v. Berrios-Berrios, 791 F.2d 246, 253–54 (2d Cir.) (remanding for statement of reasons), *cert. dismissed*, 479 U.S. 978 (1986).

III. The Crime Victims' Rights Act of 2004

The Crime Victims' Rights Act of 2004 (CVRA) was enacted October 30, 2004, and will affect a number of proceedings under the Bail Reform Act.[143] The CVRA provides crime victims certain specific rights in 18 U.S.C. § 3771(a), requires that judges ensure that the crime victim is afforded those rights in section 3771(b), and provides means by which the rights may be enforced by the victim or the government in section 3771(d). A "crime victim" is defined as a person "directly and proximately harmed as a result of the commission of a Federal offense or an offense in the District of Columbia."[144]

Among the rights provided is the right to "reasonable, accurate, and timely notice of any public court proceeding . . . involving the crime or of any release . . . of the accused."[145] This right clearly attaches at the pretrial stage, including the initial appearance and hearings involving release or detention. While the government may be in the best position to identify victims and to provide notice of proceedings to those victims, section 3771(b) could be read to give the judge some responsibility to verify that such notice has been given.[146]

Victims also have the right not to be excluded from public court proceedings except in certain circumstances.[147] Courts must make every effort to permit the fullest possible attendance by victims, and if victims are excluded, courts must clearly state the reasons on the record.[148] Victims also have the right to be "reasonably heard" at any public proceeding in the district court that involves the release, plea, or sentence of the defendant.[149] The Ninth Circuit has held that the right to be reasonably heard requires that victims be given the right to

---

143. Justice for All Act of 2004, Pub. L. No. 108-405, Title I, § 102(a), 118 Stat. 2261 (Oct. 30, 2004).
144. 18 U.S.C. § 3771(e).
145. *Id.* § 3771(a)(2).
146. *See* United States v. Turner, 367 F. Supp. 2d 319, 323–24 (E D.N.Y. 2005).
147. 18 U.S.C. § 3771(a)(3).
148. *Id.* § 3771(b).
149. *Id.* § 3771(a)(4).

speak at the hearing.[150] Victims have the right to proceedings free from unreasonable delay.[151] Victims also have the right to be reasonably protected from the accused,[152] and to be treated with fairness and with respect to their dignity and privacy.[153]

IV. Modification of Detention Order

A. Changed Circumstances

Section 3142(f) expressly authorizes reopening the detention hearing when material information "that was not known to the movant at the time of the hearing" comes to light. Thus, the D.C. Circuit upheld the reopening of a detention hearing when the government sought to put in evidence a ruling on a suppression motion made after the original hearing.[154] However, courts have interpreted this provision strictly, holding that hearings should not be reopened if the evidence was available at the time of the hearing.[155]

B. Length of Detention

Speedy Trial Act deadlines limit the length of pretrial detention. As a result of excludable-time provisions, however, defendants in complex cases may be detained far beyond the theoretical ninety-day maximum under the Speedy Trial Act, thus giving rise to due process concerns.

---

150. Kenna v. United States Dist. Ct. for the C. Dist. of Cal., 435 F.3d 1011, 1016, 1018 (9th Cir. 2006). *Accord* United States v. Degenhardt, 405 F. Supp. 2d 1341, 1345–51 (D. Utah 2005). *But see* United States v. Marcello, 370 F. Supp. 2d 745, 748 (N.D. Ill. 2005); United States v. Turner, 367 F. Supp. 2d 319, 333 (E.D.N.Y. 2005).
151. 18 U.S.C. § 3771(a)(7).
152. *Id.* § 3771(a)(1).
153. *Id.* § 3771(a)(8).
154. United States v. Peralta, 849 F.2d 625, 626–27 (D.C. Cir. 1988) (per curiam).
155. *See* United States v. Dillon, 938 F.2d 1412, 1415 (1st Cir. 1991) (holding district court's refusal to reopen detention hearing not in error where information in affidavits and letters appellant sought to present was available to him at time of hearing) (relying on United States v. Hare, 873 F.2d 796, 799 (5th Cir. 1989) (affirming refusal to reopen hearing because "testimony of Hare's family and friends is not new evidence")).

As noted in Part II, the Supreme Court has left open the possibility that detention could become so long that it would violate the defendant's substantive due process rights.[156] A number of circuit courts acknowledge that lengthy periods of detention may implicate due process concerns.[157] They appear to agree that there is no bright-line time limit for determining if the defendant has been denied due process, and that courts must decide on a case-by-case basis in light of all the circumstances.[158] The Supreme Court, in *United States v. Salerno*, indicated that the point at which the length of detention becomes constitutionally excessive is the point at which the length of detention exceeds the regulatory goals set by Congress.[159] This inquiry requires that courts balance those regulatory goals, and how the detention at issue furthers those goals, against the length of detention. However, no one analytical process or processes appear to have been established by the courts of appeals to aid courts in conducting this balancing in individual cases.

The factors to be considered in such a balancing, however, have been discussed by the courts of appeals. They include some of the factors relevant in the original detention decision—the seriousness of the charges, the strength of the government's case, the risk of flight or dangerousness to the community—as well as others unique to the due process inquiry. The first of these is the length of time the defendant has been in custody as well as the length of time he or she is expected to remain in custody before trial. This factor, while important, is rarely dispositive.[160] Another very important factor is the extent to which the prosecution bears responsibility for the delay.[161] The strength of the evidence upon which the detention is based is the third additional fac-

---

156. *See* United States v. Salerno, 481 U.S. 739 (1987).
157. United States v. El-Hage, 213 F.3d 74 (2d Cir. 2000); United States v. Infelise, 934 F.2d 103, 104 (7th Cir. 1991); United States v. Tortora, 922 F.2d 880, 889 (1st Cir. 1990); United States v. Hare, 873 F.2d 796, 799 (5th Cir. 1989); United States v. Gelfuso, 838 F.2d 358, 359 (9th Cir. 1988); United States v. Accetturo, 783 F.2d 382, 388 (3d Cir. 1986), United States v. Ojeda Rios, 846 F.2d 167, 169 (2d Cir. 1986).
158. *See, e.g., Ojeda Rios*, 846 F.2d at 169.
159. 481 U.S. 739, 747 n.4 (1987).
160. United States v. Millan, 4 F.3d 1038, 1044 (2d Cir. 1993), *cert. denied*, 511 U.S. 1011 (1994).
161. United States v. Gonzales Claudio, 806 F.2d 334, 341 (2d Cir.), *cert. dismissed*, 479 U.S. 978 (1986).

tor. Though it is a factor in the initial decision to detain, the gravity of the charges can be a particularly important factor in the determination of the constitutionality of a lengthy detention. In *United States v. El-Hage*, for example, the court found that the defendant, who was charged with offenses in connection with terrorist activity, was a "substantial threat to national security interests."[162]

A few circuits are more specific regarding how these factors are considered. The Seventh Circuit has suggested that the defendant cannot make a case that his or her detention is unconstitutional unless he or she can show that the prosecution, or the court, is unnecessarily delaying the trial regardless of the length of delay.[163] The Ninth Circuit does not go this far, but it does focus the due process inquiry on "the length of confinement in conjunction with the extent to which the prosecution bears responsibility for the delay."[164] The Fifth Circuit requires that the judicial officer determining a due process challenge consider the length of detention, the nonspeculative nature of future detention, the complexity of the case, and whether the strategy of one side or the other occasions the delay.[165]

The Seventh Circuit has noted that the remedy for an excessively long period of pretrial detention is not dismissal on due process or double jeopardy grounds. The proper remedy is review of the detention order.[166] After a defendant's conviction, the claim that pretrial detention violated due process is moot.[167] Of course, a defendant is free to argue that unlawful pretrial detention prejudiced his or her ability to defend himself or herself.[168]

---

162. 213 F.3d 74, 80 (2d Cir. 2000). *See also* United States v. El-Gabrowny, 35 F.3d 63, 64 (2d Cir. 1994) (per curiam); United States v. Orena, 986 F.2d 628 (2d Cir. 1993).

163. United States v. Infelise, 934 F.2d 103, 104 (7th Cir. 1991). "If judge and prosecutor are doing all they reasonably can be expected to do to move the case along, and the statutory criteria for pretrial detention are satisfied, then we do not think a defendant should be allowed to maintain a constitutional challenge to that detention." *Id.* at 104.

164. United States v. Gelfuso, 838 F.2d 358, 359 (9th Cir. 1988).

165. United States v. Hare, 873 F.2d 796, 801 (5th Cir. 1989) (remanding because magistrate judge "failed to consider several of these factors").

166. United States v. Warneke, 199 F.3d 906, 908 (7th Cir. 1999).

167. Murphy v. Hunt, 455 U.S. 478, 481 (1982).

168. United States v. Vachon, 869 F.2d 653, 656 (1st Cir. 1989) (rejecting the argument on the facts of that case).

V. Revocation and Modification of Release

A. Revocation for Violation of Release Conditions

If a condition of release is violated, the government may move for a revocation of the release order.[169] After a hearing, a court may revoke release if it finds

(1) ...
   (A) probable cause to believe that the person has committed a ... crime while on release; or
   (B) clear and convincing evidence that the person has violated any other condition of release; and

(2) ...
   (A) based on the factors set forth in section 3142(g) of this title, there is no condition or combination of conditions of release that will assure that the person will not flee or pose a danger to the safety of any other person or the community; or
   (B) the person is unlikely to abide by any condition or combination of conditions of release.[170]

A finding of probable cause[171] that the person committed a felony while on release gives rise to a rebuttable presumption that no release conditions can ensure the safety of others.[172] Release will be revoked unless the defendant comes forward with evidence to overcome the presumption.[173]

If the judicial officer finds that some condition or conditions of release will ensure the defendant's appearance and the community's safety, he or she may amend the conditions in accordance with section

---

169. 18 U.S.C. § 3148(b).
170. *Id.*
171. "Probable cause" under section 3148(b)(1)(A) means "that the facts available to the judicial officer 'warrant a man of reasonable caution in the belief' that the defendant has committed a crime while on bail." United States v. Gotti, 794 F.2d 773, 777 (2d Cir. 1986). *Accord* United States v. Aron, 904 F.2d 221, 224 (5th Cir. 1990); United States v. Cook, 880 F.2d 1158, 1160 (10th Cir. 1989).
172. 18 U.S.C. § 3148(b).
173. *See* United States v. Cook, 880 F.2d 1158, 1160 (10th Cir. 1989) (reversing decision not to revoke where district court found the rebuttable presumption of dangerousness established and defendant offered no evidence to rebut it).

3142. Where the revocation hearing is precipitated by the defendant's arrest on a new charge, and the new charge is itself grounds for a detention hearing, the revocation determination is separate from the detention decision on the new charge.[174]

The Second and Fifth Circuits held that section 3148(b)(2) findings must be supported by a preponderance of the evidence.[175]

The Act does not address the nature of a section 3148 hearing or whether specific findings must be made. However, the Second Circuit has held that a section 3148 hearing and a section 3142 hearing offer the same protections.[176] As in section 3142 hearings, the government may proceed by proffer.[177] The section 3142 protections are discussed in Part II.

The authorization of sanctions under section 3148 does not preclude sanctions under Federal Rule of Criminal Procedure 46(f). That provision authorizes the court to order the forfeiture of a bail bond upon the breach of a condition of release.[178]

B. Modification or Revocation Where Defendant Has Not Violated Release Conditions

Under section 3142(c)(3), a judicial officer "may at any time amend the order to impose additional or different conditions of release." This provision recognizes "the possibility that a changed situation or new information" may come to the attention of the court.[179]

---

174. *See* United States v. McKethan, 602 F. Supp. 719, 721–22 (D.D.C. 1985).
175. *Aron*, 904 F.2d at 224; *Gotti*, 794 F.2d at 778.
176. United States v. Davis, 845 F.2d 412, 414 (2d Cir. 1988) (remanding a detention order where defendant had not been permitted to testify and present evidence and the trial court had not made explicit findings or given its reasons for revocation and detention).
177. United States v. LaFontaine, 210 F.3d 125, 130 (2d Cir. 2000).
178. United States v. Gigante, 85 F.3d 83 (2d Cir. 1996); United States v. Vaccaro, 51 F.3d 189, 191 (9th Cir. 1995).
179. S. Rep. No. 98-225, at 16 (1983), *reprinted in* 1984 U.S.C.C.A.N. 3182, 3199.

VI. Review by the District Judge

The district judge may review a magistrate judge's release order on motion by the government or the defendant,[180] but only a detainee may move the district judge to revoke or amend a magistrate judge's detention order.[181] Only the district court in the prosecuting district may reverse a release or detention order of a magistrate judge in the district of arrest.[182] Review in the prosecuting district must be before the district judge, not the magistrate judge.[183]

The review is de novo,[184] and the district judge need not defer to the magistrate judge's findings or give specific reasons for rejecting them.[185] The district judge may take additional evidence or conduct a new evidentiary hearing when appropriate.[186] Following the hearing, the district judge should explain, on the record, the reasons for his or her decision.[187]

---

180. 18 U.S.C. § 3145(a)(1), (2).

181. *Id.* § 3145(b).

182. United States v. Cisneros, 328 F.3d 610, 615 (10th Cir. 2003); United States v. El-Edwy, 272 F.3d 149 (2d Cir. 2001); United States v. Torres, 86 F.3d 1029 (11th Cir. 1996); United States v. Evans, 62 F.3d 1233 (9th Cir. 1995).

183. *See* United States v. Vega, 438 F.3d 801, 802 (7th Cir. 2006); *Cisneros*, 328 F.3d at 615; *Evans*, 62 F.3d at 1239.

184. United States v. Rueben, 974 F.2d 580, 585 (5th Cir. 1992), *cert. denied*, 507 U.S. 940 (1993); United States v. Tortora, 922 F.2d 880, 883 n.4 (1st Cir. 1990); United States v. Koenig, 912 F.2d 1190, 1191 (9th Cir. 1990); United States v. Clark, 865 F.2d 1433, 1436 (4th Cir. 1989) (en banc); United States v. King, 849 F.2d 485, 489–90 (11th Cir. 1988); United States v. Leon, 766 F.2d 77, 80 (2d Cir. 1985); United States v. Delker, 757 F.2d 1390, 1394–95 (3d Cir. 1985); United States v. Maull, 773 F.2d 1479, 1482 (8th Cir. 1985) (en banc).

185. *Koenig*, 912 F.2d at 1191–92; *Leon*, 766 F.2d at 80; *Delker*, 757 F.2d at 1394–95; United States v. Medina, 775 F.2d 1398, 1402 (11th Cir. 1985).

186. *Koenig*, 912 F.2d at 1193; *Delker*, 757 F.2d at 1393–94; United States v. Fortna, 769 F.2d 243, 250 (5th Cir. 1985) (district judge should consider record plus additional evidence). The Third Circuit advises district judges to consider whether a transcript of the proceedings before the magistrate judge will help determine if more evidence is needed. *Delker*, 757 F.2d at 1395 n.3. The Eighth Circuit has held that the district judge should have a full de novo evidentiary hearing if either side requests one. United States v. Maull, 773 F.2d 1479, 1481–82 (8th Cir. 1985) (en banc).

187. The Eleventh Circuit's rule is that the district judge may, after independent review, adopt the magistrate judge's pretrial detention order. The explicit adoption of that order eliminates the need for the district judge to prepare separate written findings of fact and a statement of reasons. United States v. King, 849 F.2d 485, 490 (11th Cir. 1988).

Review of a detention or release order shall "be determined promptly."[188] The statute does not define "promptly" or set forth a remedy for review that is not prompt. The Supreme Court has said that release is generally not the appropriate remedy for an untimely initial hearing.[189] The First Circuit held that, where the district judge "was attentive to the need for promptness, but unable to accommodate [the review] because of judicial travel commitments," delay was excusable.[190] The Ninth Circuit held that a thirty-day delay violates the requirement and that conditional release is an appropriate remedy.[191] However, in a subsequent case, the Ninth Circuit limited this holding to cases where detention is based on risk of flight. The court held that where the detention is based on danger to the community, release is not a proper remedy.[192] The Fifth Circuit agrees.[193] The Fourth Circuit has said that automatic release is not an appropriate remedy for any violation of the Act.[194]

VII. Review by the Court of Appeals

The defendant and the government may directly appeal a trial court's release order, and the defendant may appeal a detention order, without

---

188. 18 U.S.C. § 3145(a), (b).

189. United States v. Montalvo-Murillo, 495 U.S. 711, 716–17 (1990), discussed *supra* text accompanying notes 66–70.

190. United States v. Palmer-Contreras, 835 F.2d 15, 19 (1st Cir. 1987) (stating further, "in the unique circumstances of this case, . . . the judge's attendance at the judicial conference constituted good cause for delay").

191. United States v. Fernandez-Alfonso, 813 F.2d 1571, 1572 (9th Cir. 1987).

192. United States v. Gonzales, 852 F.2d 1214, 1215 (9th Cir. 1988). Because defendant sought only conditional release, the court left open the question "whether there are other remedies for a district court's failure to determine promptly a motion for revocation of a detention order when the defendant poses a danger to the community."

193. United States v. Barker, 876 F.2d 475, 476 (5th Cir. 1989).

194. United States v. Clark, 865 F.2d 1433, 1436 (4th Cir. 1989) (en banc) ("in cases where the requirements of the Bail Reform Act are not properly met, automatic release is not the appropriate remedy").

first seeking reconsideration in the trial court. Such appeals are to be determined promptly.[195]

The courts of appeals differ on the standard for reviewing trial court determinations under the Bail Reform Act. Though the articulation of the standards varies from circuit to circuit, the various statements of those standards may be summarized into three approaches. The Second, Fourth, and Fifth Circuits are the most deferential to the determinations of the district courts. The Second Circuit has indicated that it will examine the district courts' determinations for "clear error."[196] This deference is applicable to the courts' overall determination as well as specific factual determinations.[197] The Fourth Circuit's "clearly erroneous" standard is similar.[198] The Fifth Circuit will affirm the district court's determination "if it is supported by the proceedings below."[199]

The First and Third Circuits take an intermediate approach. The First undertakes an independent review, but with some deference to the determinations made by the district court. This level of scrutiny is "more rigorous than the abuse-of-discretion or clear-error standards, but stopping short of plenary or *de novo* review."[200] The First Circuit emphasizes that the scope of review is less deferential if the district court does not provide detailed reasons for its decision.[201] The court of appeals is free to consider material not presented in the district

---

195. 18 U.S.C. § 3145(c). Section 3145(c) incorporates by reference the provisions of 18 U.S.C. § 3731 ("Appeal by the United States:" government may appeal a decision granting the release of a defendant or denying a motion for revocation or modification of release) and 28 U.S.C. § 1291. Such appeals are governed by Rule 9 of the Federal Rules of Appellate Procedure.
196. United States v. Ferranti, 66 F.3d 540, 542 (2d Cir. 1995). *See also* United States v. Chimurenga, 760 F.2d 400, 405 (2d Cir. 1985). If a district court's findings raise constitutional issues, they are reviewed de novo. United States v. Millan, 4 F.3d 1038, 1043 (2d Cir. 1993).
197. United States v. Berrios-Berrios, 791 F.2d 246, 247 (2d Cir. 1986).
198. United States v. Clark, 865 F.2d 1433, 1437 (4th Cir. 1989) (en banc).
199. United States v. Aron, 904 F.2d 221, 223 (5th Cir. 1990) (quoting United States v. Barker, 876 F.2d 475, 476 (5th Cir. 1989)). The Fifth Circuit has also equated its "narrow standard of review . . . to the abuse of discretion standard." United States v. Araneda, 899 F.2d 368, 370 (5th Cir. 1990) (quoting United States v. Jackson, 845 F.2d 1262, 1263 (5th Cir. 1988)).
200. United States v. Tortora, 922 F.2d 880, 883 (1st Cir. 1990).
201. *Id.*

court.[202] Similarly, the Third Circuit undertakes an independent review while giving "respectful consideration" to the lower court's determination.[203]

The Sixth, Seventh, Eighth, Ninth, Tenth, and Eleventh Circuits are the least deferential to the district courts' determinations. They review de novo the district court's ultimate determination (although they defer to particular findings of fact).[204]

VIII. Release or Detention Pending Sentence

Section 3143(a) governs the release or detention of defendants "found guilty" and awaiting imposition or execution of a sentence of imprisonment. Neither section 3143(a) nor any other provision covers situations in which the Sentencing Guidelines do not recommend a term of imprisonment.[205] All convicted defendants, except those convicted of crimes of violence, offenses with a maximum sentence of life imprisonment or death, or certain drug-related offenses carrying a maximum term of ten years or more, must be detained unless the judicial officer finds by clear and convincing evidence that the person is not likely to flee or pose a danger to the safety of any other person or the community if released.[206] For release to be in order, then, the judicial officer must find both nonlikelihood of flight and nondangerousness.[207] Release is made in accordance with section 3142.

---

202. Fed. R. App. P. 9(a); United States v. Patriarca, 948 F.2d 789, 795 n.6 (1st Cir. 1991); *Tortora*, 922 F.2d at 883; United States v. O'Brien, 895 F.2d 810, 814 (1st Cir. 1990).

203. *See* United States v. Delker, 757 F.2d 1390, 1399 (3d Cir. 1985); United States v. Traitz, 807 F.2d 322, 325 (3d Cir. 1986).

204. *See, e.g.,* United States v. Cantu, 935 F.2d 950, 951 (8th Cir. 1991); United States v. Townsend, 897 F.2d 989, 994 (9th Cir. 1990); United States v. Montalvo-Murillo, 876 F.2d 826, 830 (10th Cir. 1989), *rev'd on other grounds,* 495 U.S. 711 (1990); United States v. Portes, 786 F.2d 758, 762 (7th Cir. 1985); United States v. Hurtado, 779 F.2d 1467, 1472 (11th Cir. 1985); United States v. Hazime, 762 F.2d 34, 37 (6th Cir. 1985).

205. In *United States v. Booker*, 543 U.S. 220 (2005), the Supreme Court held that the Sentencing Guidelines are advisory. Judges must therefore consult the Guidelines, but are not bound by them.

206. 18 U.S.C. § 3143(a)(1).

207. *See* United States v. Manso-Portes, 838 F.2d 889, 889–90 (7th Cir. 1987).

Generally, defendants convicted of crimes of violence, offenses with a maximum sentence of life imprisonment or death, or drug-related offenses carrying a maximum term of ten or more years—crimes listed in sections 3142(f)(1)(A), (B), and (C)—must be detained unless the judicial officer finds (1) "a substantial likelihood that a motion for acquittal or new trial will be granted," or the government recommends that imprisonment not be imposed; and (2) "by clear and convincing evidence that the person is not likely to flee or pose a danger to any other person or the community."[208]

The Fifth and Tenth Circuits held that defendants detained under section 3143(a)(2) may be released if the findings of section 3143(a)(1) on flight and danger are met; and there are "exceptional reasons," under the provision of section 3145(c), as to why the defendant should be released.[209]

The Sixth Circuit found it error to release a convicted defendant without holding a hearing simply because the court believed that he was not dangerous; the government was entitled to an opportunity to respond to the defendant's evidence and offer its own.[210] The Seventh Circuit has gone further and interpreted section 3143 as establishing a rebuttable presumption of dangerousness, maintaining that the "clear and convincing" standard cannot be met if the defendant offers no evidence, even if the court does not believe the defendant is dangerous.[211]

The Second and Sixth Circuits have criticized district courts that relied too much on a defendant's demeanor or the opinions of family members concerning risk of flight or dangerousness.[212]

As with pretrial detention, dangerousness under section 3143 is not limited to physical danger.[213]

---

208. 18 U.S.C. § 3143(a)(2).
209. United States v. Jones, 979 F.2d 804, 806 (10th Cir. 1992) (per curiam); United States v. Carr, 947 F.2d 1239, 1240 (5th Cir. 1992) (per curiam) (holding 18 U.S.C. § 3145(c) applies).
210. United States v. Vance, 851 F.2d 166, 168 (6th Cir.), *cert. denied,* 488 U.S. 893 (1988).
211. *Manso-Portes*, 838 F.2d at 890.
212. United States v. London-Villa, 898 F.2d 328, 330 (2d Cir. 1990); *Vance*, 851 F.2d at 168. *See supra* note 36, concerning same point in connection with initial detention decision.
213. The legislative history specifically mentions drug trafficking as a danger to the community. *See* S. Rep. No. 98-225, at 12–13 (1983), *reprinted in* 1984 U.S.C.C.A.N. 3182, 3195–96. *See also Manso-Portes*, 838 F.2d at 890 (holding section 3143 applies to drug offenders).

The Second Circuit held that, for the purposes of section 3143(a), a defendant is "found guilty" the moment a jury returns a guilty verdict, even before the court has entered judgment.[214] Once the defendant has filed an appeal, release under this section is no longer appropriate and section 3143(b) applies.

Legislative history suggests that section 3143(a) covers those awaiting "execution" of a sentence in order to make clear that a person may be released for a short period after sentencing "for such matters as getting his affairs in order prior to surrendering for service of sentence."[215]

The Seventh Circuit held that release pursuant to section 3143(a) is improper if the defendant awaits resentencing not because of an infirmity in the original sentence, but because the vacation of a concurrent sentence might lead the sentencing judge to reconsider a sentence not vacated.[216]

IX. Release or Detention Pending Appeal

A. Release Requirements

A defendant who has been sentenced for a crime not listed in section 3142(f)(1)(A), (B), or (C)—crimes of violence, offenses carrying a maximum sentence of life imprisonment or death, or drug offenses carrying a maximum sentence of ten years or more—and who is pursuing an appeal or a petition for certiorari[217] must be detained unless the judicial officer finds that the defendant is not likely to flee or pose a danger to the community and "that the appeal is not for the purpose of delay and raises a substantial question of law or fact likely to result in"

---

214. United States v. Bloomer, 967 F.2d 761, 763 (2d Cir. 1992).
215. S. Rep. No. 98-225, at 26 (1983), *reprinted in* 1984 U.S.C.C.A.N. 3182, 3209.
216. United States v. Holzer, 848 F.2d 822, 824 (7th Cir.), *cert. denied*, 488 U.S. 928 (1988).
217. In *United States v. Snyder*, 946 F.2d 1125, 1126 (5th Cir. 1991), the Fifth Circuit held that the district court, court of appeals, and Supreme Court have concurrent jurisdiction to decide whether to release a defendant on bail while a petition for certiorari is pending.

reversal, a new trial, or a sentence of no imprisonment or imprisonment less than the time already served.[218]

If a defendant is appealing conviction for a crime that is listed in subsection (A), (B), or (C), detention is mandatory[219] unless the judicial officer finds no risk of flight or danger and a "substantial question" *and* finds that "there are exceptional reasons why such person's detention would not be appropriate."[220]

If the government is appealing a sentence of imprisonment, but the defendant is not, the defendant shall be detained during the appeal.[221]

If release is based on a likelihood of reversal, the court must find a likelihood of reversal on all counts for which imprisonment was imposed.[222]

The burden is on the defendant to show that the criteria for release are met.[223] Section 3143(b)(1)(A) explicitly states that nonlikelihood of fleeing and nondangerousness must be established by clear and convincing evidence.[224] It does not address the standards for determining that the appeal is not for the purpose of delay and that the appeal raises a substantial question pursuant to section 3143(b)(1)(B). The

---

218. 18 U.S.C. § 3143(b)(1)(B).

219. *Id.* § 3143(b)(2).

220. *Id.* § 3145(c). *See also* United States v. Herrera-Soto, 961 F.2d 645, 646 (7th Cir. 1992) (section 3145(c) not limited to appeals of detention orders); United States v. DiSomma, 951 F.2d 494, 496 (2d Cir. 1991) (same).

221. 18 U.S.C. § 3143(c).

222. Morison v. United States, 486 U.S. 1306 (1987) (denying application for release because, although defendant raised substantial question with respect to his conviction on one count, he did not do so with respect to all counts for which imprisonment was imposed).

223. United States v. Montoya, 908 F.2d 450, 451 (9th Cir. 1990); United States v. Smith, 793 F.2d 85, 87–88 (3d Cir. 1986), *cert. denied,* 479 U.S. 1031 (1987); United States v. Randell, 761 F.2d 122, 125 (2d Cir.), *cert. denied,* 474 U.S. 1008 (1985); United States v. Miller, 753 F.2d 19, 24 (3d Cir. 1985); United States v. Crabtree, 754 F.2d 1200, 1201 (5th Cir.), *cert. denied,* 473 U.S. 905 (1985); United States v. Valera-Elizondo, 761 F.2d 1020, 1025 (5th Cir. 1985); United States v. Bilanzich, 771 F.2d 292, 298 (7th Cir. 1985); United States v. Powell, 761 F.2d 1227, 1232 (8th Cir. 1985) (en banc) (burden of showing merit of appeal); United States v. Handy, 761 F.2d 1279, 1283 (9th Cir. 1985); United States v. Affleck, 765 F.2d 944, 953 (10th Cir. 1985) (en banc); United States v. Giancola, 754 F.2d 898, 900–01 (11th Cir. 1985) (per curiam).

224. 18 U.S.C. § 3143(b)(1)(A).

Tenth Circuit, the only circuit to address this question, held that the "preponderance of evidence" standard applies.[225]

The district court must state on the record its reasons for denying release pending appeal.[226] The statement of reasons may be made either through written findings or through a transcript of an oral statement.[227] Noting the injustice of a defendant's prevailing on appeal only after serving most of a sentence, the Seventh Circuit urges district courts to "stat[e] in detail their reasons for denying a petition for release pending appeal, especially in a case . . . in which the defendants posed no danger to the community and apparently negligible threat of flight."[228]

Section 3143(b) applies only to a defendant "who has filed an appeal or a petition for a writ of certiorari."[229] It does not apply to defendants seeking post-conviction relief.[230] Thus, the D.C. Circuit held that release is not available pending appeal of the denial of a motion for a new trial made pursuant to Federal Rule of Criminal Procedure 33.[231]

When a defendant is awaiting resentencing after an original sentence has been vacated, and the defendant has filed a petition for certiorari, the Seventh Circuit has held that section 3143(b) and not 3143(a) controls release. The court cautioned that "[a]n imprisoned person is not to be released pending further proceedings if it is a cer-

---

225. *Affleck*, 765 F.2d at 953 n.15. *See also* United States v. Galanis, 695 F. Supp. 1565, 1566 (S.D.N.Y. 1988) (stating "defendant must show by a preponderance of the evidence, that his 'appeal is not for purpose of delay and it raises a substantial question of law or fact likely to result in reversal or an order for a new trial'") (quoting 18 U.S.C. § 3143(b)(2), which has since been renumbered as section 3143(b)(1)(B) pursuant to amendment in 1990); United States v. Delanoy, 867 F. Supp. 114, 116 (N.D N.Y. 1994) (stating section 3143(b)(1)(B) "must be analyzed under a preponderance of the evidence standard").

226. Fed. R. App. P. 9(b); United States v. Wheeler, 795 F.2d 839, 840–41 (9th Cir. 1986) (remanding for statement of reasons).

227. *Wheeler*, 795 F.2d at 841.

228. United States v. Harris, 942 F.2d 1125, 1135 n.7 (7th Cir. 1991). The court also urged counsel who believe their clients' petition for release should have been granted to renew the petition in their appellate briefs.

229. 18 U.S.C. § 3143(b).

230. Cherek v. United States, 767 F.2d 335, 337 (7th Cir. 1985).

231. United States v. Kelly, 790 F.2d 130, 139 (D.C. Cir. 1986).

tainty that however those proceedings are resolved, he will have to be returned to prison."[232]

B. Definitions of "Substantial Question" and "Likely"[233]

The definition of "substantial question of law or fact" varies slightly among the circuits. Most circuits define it as "a 'close' question or one that very well could be decided the other way."[234] The Ninth Circuit declined to endorse the "close" question standard, holding instead that the question must be "fairly debatable."[235] The Third Circuit has indicated its preference for the "fairly debatable" criterion.[236]

The requirement that the substantial question be "likely" to result in reversal, a new trial, or a sentence without imprisonment is not as straightforward as it may seem. The Third Circuit rejected the literal

---

232. United States v. Krilich, 178 F.3d 859, 926 (7th Cir. 1999). See also *United States v. Lagiglio*, 384 F.3d 925 (7th Cir. 2004), where, in a decision after the Seventh Circuit decision in *United States v. Booker*, 375 F.3d 508 (7th Cir. 2004), but before that decision was affirmed, 543 U.S. 220 (2005), the court remanded the issue of resentencing to the district court to determine, under section 3143(b), whether it was likely that a new sentence would already be served by the time the appeal was resolved.

233. Although the likelihood of prevailing on appeal is, by the terms of the statute, applicable only to determinations of release pending appeal, not determinations of release pending sentencing, the First Circuit has held that in the latter context it may be relevant to the issue of likelihood of flight. United States v. Castiello, 878 F.2d 554, 555 (1st Cir. 1989) (per curiam).

234. United States v. Giancola, 754 F.2d 898, 901 (11th Cir. 1985) (per curiam); United States v. Eaken, 995 F.2d 740, 741 (7th Cir. 1993); United States v. Steinhorn, 927 F.2d 195, 196 (4th Cir. 1991); United States v. Perholtz, 836 F.2d 554, 555 (D.C. Cir. 1987) (per curiam), *cert. denied*, 488 U.S. 923 (1988); United States v. Bayko, 774 F.2d 516, 523 (1st Cir. 1985); United States v. Affleck, 765 F.2d 944, 952 (10th Cir. 1985) (en banc); United States v. Randell, 761 F.2d 122, 125 (2d Cir.), *cert. denied*, 474 U.S. 1008 (1985); United States v. Valera-Elizondo, 761 F.2d 1020, 1024 (5th Cir. 1985); United States v. Pollard, 778 F.2d 1177, 1182 (6th Cir. 1985); United States v. Powell, 761 F.2d 1227, 1231 (8th Cir. 1985) (en banc).

235. United States v. Handy, 761 F.2d 1279, 1281–83 (9th Cir. 1985). In a subsequent case, the Ninth Circuit held that the defendant must do more than identify the argument he or she intends to make in support of an appeal; the defendant must explain the basis for that argument and give at least some indication of why the argument is likely to prevail. United States v. Montoya, 908 F.2d 450, 450–51 (9th Cir. 1990).

236. United States v. Smith, 793 F.2d 85, 89–90 (3d Cir. 1986), *cert. denied*, 479 U.S. 1031 (1987). An earlier Third Circuit case, *United States v. Miller*, 753 F.2d 19, 23 (3d Cir. 1985), defined a "substantial question" as "one which is . . . novel, which has not been decided by controlling precedent, or which is fairly doubtful." In *Smith*, 793 F.2d at 87–89, the court stressed that the question must also be "significant."

interpretation, which implies that a court should grant bail pending appeal only if it finds its own rulings likely to be reversed,[237] and held that the "likely" requirement is met as long as the substantial "question is so integral to the merits of the conviction on which defendant is to be imprisoned that a contrary appellate holding is likely to require reversal of the conviction."[238] If the alleged error would be deemed harmless error, or was not adequately preserved for appeal, it does not meet this requirement.[239] Several courts have adopted the Third Circuit's approach.[240] Other courts have held that a determination that the defendant's appeal is "likely" to result in reversal, a new trial, or a sentence without imprisonment means this result is "more probable than not."[241] The Seventh Circuit specifies that "§ 3143(b) 'requires an affirmative finding that the chance for reversal is substantial. . . . [A] conviction is presumed to be correct.'"[242]

C. "Exceptional Reasons"

Defendants convicted of certain crimes, or crimes carrying certain sentences, must be detained absent "exceptional reasons" why their detention is inappropriate.[243] The Second Circuit has noted that because the "legislative history on the issue [of what constitutes exceptional reasons] is sparse and uninformative," a "case by case evaluation is essential" with broad discretion given to the trial judge.[244] The court defined

---

237. *Miller*, 753 F.2d at 23.
238. *Id.*
239. *Id.*
240. United States v. Bayko, 774 F.2d 516, 522 (1st Cir. 1985); United States v. Randell, 761 F.2d 122, 125 (2d Cir.), *cert. denied*, 474 U.S. 1008 (1985); United States v. Affleck, 765 F.2d 944, 953 (10th Cir. 1985) (en banc); United States v. Giancola, 754 F.2d 898, 900 (11th Cir. 1985) (per curiam).
241. United States v. Valera-Elizondo, 761 F.2d 1020, 1025 (5th Cir. 1985); United States v. Pollard, 778 F.2d 1177, 1182 (6th Cir. 1985); United States v. Bilanzich, 771 F.2d 292, 299 (7th Cir. 1985); United States v. Powell, 761 F.2d 1227, 1233 (8th Cir. 1985) (en banc).
242. United States v. Ashman, 964 F.2d 596, 599 (7th Cir. 1992), *cert. denied sub nom.* Barcal v. United States, 510 U.S. 814 (1993) (quoting United States v. Bilanzich, 771 F.2d 292, 298 (7th Cir. 1985)).
243. 18 U.S.C. § 3145(c).
244. United States v. DiSomma, 951 F.2d 494, 497 (2d Cir. 1991). *Accord* United States v. Herrera-Soto, 961 F.2d 645, 647 (7th Cir. 1992).

exceptional circumstances as a "unique combination of circumstances giving rise to situations that are out of the ordinary."[245] The court upheld a district court's determination that exceptional circumstances were present where the defendant's appeal challenged the very element of the crime that entailed the "violence" justifying detention. In another case, the Second Circuit reversed a district court's finding that exceptional circumstances existed because the defendant was employed full time and was a college student with no prior convictions. The court found that such circumstances were not exceptional and, citing a district court case that had collected and discussed a great many of the cases in this area, noted that "circumstances that are 'purely personal' do not typically rise to the level of 'exceptional' warranting release."[246]

X. Release or Detention of a Material Witness

A material witness is subject to detention if certain conditions, including the inadequacy of preserving the witness's testimony through deposition, are met.[247] Section 3144 provides that a material witness be treated in accordance with the provisions of section 3142. According to one district court, that directive includes a right to appointed counsel if the witness is unable to retain counsel.[248] The Second Circuit has held that section 3144 applies to grand jury proceedings.[249]

---

245. *DiSomma*, 951 F.2d at 497.
246. United States v. Lea, 360 F.3d 401, 403 (2d Cir. 2004) (quoting with approval United States v. Lippold, 175 F. Supp. 2d 537, 540 (S.D.N.Y. 2001)). *See also* United States v. Mostrom, 11 F.3d 93 (2d Cir. 1993).
247. 18 U.S.C. § 3144.
248. *See In re* Class Action Application for Habeas Corpus on Behalf of All Material Witnesses in the W. Dist. of Tex., 612 F. Supp. 940, 942–43 (W.D. Tex. 1985).
249. United States v. Awadallah, 349 F.3d 42, 49 (2d Cir. 2003).

XI. Release or Detention Pending Revocation of Probation or Supervised Release

The Bail Reform Act does not specifically address the issue of bail pending hearings on violations of probation and supervised release. The provisions of section 3143, however, are incorporated by reference. Rule 32.1(a)(1) of the Federal Rules of Criminal Procedure provides that a defendant may be released pursuant to Rule 46(c) pending a revocation hearing. Rule 46(c), in turn, provides that section 3143 governs eligibility of release pending sentence or pending notice of appeal. Read together, these provisions stipulate that the standards applicable to release pending sentence are applicable to defendants facing revocation of probation or supervised release.[250]

XII. Offense Committed While on Bail

Under 18 U.S.C. § 3147, a person convicted of another offense while released under the Bail Reform Act shall receive up to a ten-year term of imprisonment if the offense is a felony and up to one year if a misdemeanor, to run consecutively with the sentence imposed for the original offense.[251] In a Ninth Circuit case,[252] the defendant pled guilty to several offenses committed while on release and one that was not committed while on release. The latter carried the longest sentence, fifty-one months. The sentences were imposed concurrently, totaling fifty-one months, with a section 3147 enhancement of fourteen months to run consecutively. The defendant argued that section 3147 enhancements should run consecutively only to sentences for offenses committed during release on bail. The court disagreed: "The plain

---

250. United States v. Loya, 23 F.3d 1529 (9th Cir. 1994).

251. In *Rodriguez v. United States*, 480 U.S. 522 (1987) (per curiam), the Supreme Court held that this term of imprisonment may be suspended and probation imposed under 18 U.S.C. § 3651. However, the Sentencing Reform Act of 1984 repealed section 3651, and the Supreme Court decision applies only to offenses committed before Nov. 1, 1987.

252. United States v. Galliano, 977 F.2d 1350 (9th Cir. 1992), *cert. denied,* 507 U.S. 966 (1993).

language of section 3147(1) requires the enhancement term to run consecutively to any other sentence of imprisonment regardless of when the underlying offense was committed."[253]

The Fifth Circuit clarified that a section 3147 enhancement applies to the sentence for the new crime committed while on release, not to the original crime for which the defendant was on release.[254] The Fifth Circuit also noted that section 3147 applies only to federal offenses committed while the defendant is on release, not to state offenses.[255]

The Fourth and Sixth Circuits have held that a defendant who fails to appear in violation of the provisions of 18 U.S.C. § 3146 is subject to an enhancement under section 3147.[256] The Sixth Circuit rejected the defendant's argument that such an interpretation of section 3147 amounted to a violation of the Double Jeopardy Clause.[257]

Noting section 3142(h)(2)(A)'s requirement that a releasing judge notify a person of "the penalties for violating a condition of release, including the penalties for committing an offense while on pretrial release," the Fourth, Fifth, and Seventh Circuits held that imposition of an additional sentence pursuant to section 3147 is improper if the defendant was not notified of the possibility of such a penalty when released on bail.[258] The Third, Sixth, and Ninth Circuits disagree, and have held that section 3147 does not incorporate the notice requirements of section 3142.[259]

---

253. *Id.* at 1351.
254. United States v. Pace, 955 F.2d 270, 278–79 (5th Cir. 1992).
255. *Id.*
256. United States v. Fitzgerald, 435 F.3d 484 (4th Cir. 2006); United States v. Benson, 134 F.3d 787 (6th Cir. 1998).
257. *Fitzgerald*, 435 F.3d at 487.
258. United States v. Onick, 889 F.2d 1425, 1433–34 (5th Cir. 1989); United States v. DiCaro, 852 F.2d 259, 264–65 (7th Cir. 1988); United States v. Cooper, 827 F.2d 991, 994–95 (4th Cir. 1987).
259. United States v. Kentz, 251 F.3d 835, 840 (9th Cir.), *cert. denied,* 535 U.S. 933 (2001); United States v. Lewis, 991 F.2d 322, 323 (6th Cir. 1993); United States v. DiPasquale, 864 F.2d 271, 280–81 (3d Cir. 1988), *cert. denied sub nom.* Cohen v. United States, 492 U.S. 906 (1989). The Second Circuit suggested that it would be inclined to agree with the Third and Sixth Circuits but did not have to reach the issue because the defendant had received notice. United States v. Vasquez, 113 F.3d 383, 390 (2d Cir.), *cert. denied sub nom.* Peralta v. United States, 522 U.S. 900 (1997).

A number of defendants have protested their enhanced sentences, arguing that section 3147 establishes an independent offense for which they cannot be punished absent separate indictment and trial. The courts have rejected that contention, holding that section 3147 is a sentence-enhancement provision; it does not establish a separate offense.[260]

This issue arose anew after the Supreme Court's decision in *Apprendi v. New Jersey*.[261] The defendants argued that the pre-*Apprendi* characterizations of sentencing factors and elements of the offense were no longer controlling and that section 3147 establishes a sentencing enhancement that requires the charging and proof of facts that increase the sentence above the otherwise applicable maximum. Courts that have considered this issue, however, have held that the Sentencing Commission has essentially mooted the argument.[262] Section 2J1.7 of the Sentencing Guidelines encourages judges to sentence within the guideline range for the base offense of conviction (accordingly, within the statutory maximum for the new offense) and to use the section 3147 enhancement only to determine where a sentence should be imposed within that range. Sentencing in accordance with the Guidelines has not, therefore, been found to have resulted in an enhancement that falls within the concerns of *Apprendi*. Given the reliance courts have placed on section 2J1.7 of the Guidelines as authority for the enhancement, it may be anticipated that new challenges will arise as a result of *United States v. Booker*,[263] which held that the Guidelines are not binding on the court.

---

260. United States v. Jackson, 891 F.2d 1151, 1152–53 (5th Cir. 1989), *cert. denied*, 496 U.S. 939 (1990); *DiPasquale*, 864 F.2d at 279–80; United States v. Feldhacker, 849 F.2d 293, 298–99 (8th Cir. 1988); United States v. Patterson, 820 F.2d 1524, 1526–27 (9th Cir. 1987).

261. 530 U.S. 466 (2000).

262. United States v. Samuel, 296 F.3d 1169 (D.C. Cir.), *cert denied*, 537 U.S. 1078 (2002); United States v. Randall, 287 F.3d 27, 30 (1st Cir.), *cert. denied*, 537 U.S. 916 (2002). Several courts have also refused to reverse sentences under section 3147 because the complete sentence did not exceed the maximum statutory sentence for the base offense. *See* United States v. Gillon, 348 F.3d 755, 758 (8th Cir. 2003); *Kentz*, 251 F.3d at 844; United States v. Ellis, 241 F.3d 1096, 1103 (9th Cir. 2001); United States v. Parolin, 239 F.3d 922, 929 (7th Cir.), *cert. denied*, 533 U.S. 923 (2001).

263. 543 U.S. 220 (2005).

XIII. Sanctions

A. Failure to Appear

Section 3146 specifies the sanctions, including fines, imprisonment, and forfeiture, for failure to appear in court and failure to surrender for service of sentence.[264] Under section 3146(c), "uncontrollable circumstances" not caused by the defendant is an affirmative defense, provided the person appeared or surrendered as soon as the circumstances ceased to exist.

Courts require the failure to appear to be "willful" or "knowing."[265] However, the Tenth Circuit has twice sustained convictions where defendants lacked actual notice of the court proceeding in question.[266] In one case, the defendant, a fugitive for an extended period, claimed he did not knowingly fail to appear on the date in question because he only subsequently learned the date. Finding that failure to appear is a continuing offense, the court held that the government need not prove an exact date for the completed offense and that the defendant should have contacted the court.[267] The Tenth Circuit rejected another defendant's contention that his failure to appear could not be willful because he never received notice of the proceeding: the defendant "was a fugitive as soon as he failed to comply with the terms of the supervised release and absented himself. . . . [He] made no attempt to contact his attorney or the court. . . . Under these circumstances no actual notice to the defendant was necessary. The notice to his attorney was sufficient."[268] In a somewhat analogous situation, the Ninth Circuit held that failure to appear on the date set for trial was a violation even though the defendant had been given conflicting information about

---

264. *See* 18 U.S.C. § 3146(b), (d).
265. *See, e.g.,* United States v. Simmons, 912 F.2d 1215, 1217 (10th Cir. 1990); United States v. Martinez, 890 F.2d 1088, 1091 (10th Cir. 1989), *cert. denied,* 494 U.S. 1059 (1990). *See also* 18 U.S.C. § 3146(c) (affirmative defenses listed).
266. *Simmons,* 912 F.2d at 1217; *Martinez,* 890 F.2d at 1091.
267. *Martinez,* 890 F.2d at 1091–93.
268. *Simmons,* 912 F.2d at 1217.

that date because he "engage[d] in a course of conduct designed to avoid notice of his trial date."[269]

The Sixth, Seventh, Eighth, and Eleventh Circuits have rejected the claim that double jeopardy prohibits prosecution under section 3146 where the failure to appear was already the basis for an enhancement of the sentence for the original offense.[270]

The Sixth and Seventh Circuits held that when a court in one district orders a defendant to appear before a court in another district, either court has jurisdiction over a prosecution for failure to appear.[271]

B. Contempt

In addition to revocation of release, discussed in Part I, contempt proceedings may be initiated against a person who violates a release condition.[272]

XIV. Credit Toward Detention

Section 3585(b) of the Sentencing Reform Act gives a defendant credit toward the term of imprisonment for time spent in official detention before the commencement of the sentence (1) for the offense for which the sentence was imposed, or (2) for any other charge for which the defendant was arrested after he or she committed the offense for which the sentence was imposed, provided it has not been credited toward another sentence.

In *United States v. Wilson*,[273] the Supreme Court resolved a circuit split, holding that the authority to compute credit belongs to the U.S. Attorney General, who has delegated that authority to the Bureau of

---

269. Weaver v. United States, 37 F.3d 1411, 1413 (9th Cir. 1994).

270. United States v. Bolding, 972 F.2d 184, 185 (8th Cir. 1992); United States v. Carey, 943 F.2d 44, 46 (11th Cir. 1991), *cert. denied*, 112 S. Ct. 1676 (1992); United States v. Mack, 938 F.2d 678, 679–81 (6th Cir. 1991); United States v. Troxell, 887 F.2d 830, 836 (7th Cir. 1989).

271. United States v. Chappell, 854 F.2d 190, 191–93 (7th Cir. 1988), *cert. denied*, 504 U.S. 927 (1992); United States v. Williams, 788 F.2d 1213, 1214 (6th Cir. 1986).

272. 18 U.S.C. § 3148(a), (c).

273. 503 U.S. 329 (1992).

Prisons.[274] Prisoners may seek administrative review of the computation of credit and, after exhausting administrative remedies, may pursue judicial review.[275]

Another circuit split was resolved by the Supreme Court in *Reno v. Koray*.[276] There, resolving the split in favor of the majority view, the Court upheld the Bureau of Prison's policy of not crediting as "official detention" time spent in community confinement as a condition of pretrial release. "Official detention" within the meaning of section 3585(b) refers to a court's order that a defendant be detained and committed to the custody of the Attorney General for confinement. Although that case specifically involved halfway house confinement, the holding clearly covers other restrictive conditions.

In her concurring opinion in *Reno*, Justice Ginsburg suggested that due process might require a warning to a defendant that time in a halfway house, or some other restrictive condition, would not result in credit against an eventual sentence.[277] The Second Circuit, however, rejected any due process right to such a warning.[278] Nonetheless, the court noted that judicial officers might wish to volunteer such a warning.[279]

Despite the rulings placing credit decisions within the authority of the Attorney General, a few of the earlier courts of appeals decisions are worth noting. The Eleventh Circuit, in *United States v. Harris*,[280] held, in a somewhat unusual factual situation, that time spent in a state prison can be credited if the defendants can establish that federal law enforcement officials took the initiative in getting the state to take the defendants into custody. In that case, a Drug Enforcement Agency agent asked local officers to obtain and execute a search warrant after

---

274. Before the Sentencing Reform Act of 1984, the governing statute, 18 U.S.C. § 3568, explicitly gave the Attorney General this authority. The amended statute deleted this provision but did not substitute another authority to make that determination. 18 U.S.C. § 3585. In *United States v. Wilson*, 503 U.S. 329, 335 (1992), the Supreme Court held that Congress did not intend to take the initial determination away from the Attorney General.

275. *Wilson*, 503 U.S. at 335.

276. 515 U.S. 50 (1995).

277. *Id.* at 65.

278. Cucciniello v. Keller, 137 F.3d 721, 724 (2d Cir. 1998).

279. *Id.* at 725.

280. 876 F.2d 1502 (11th Cir.), *cert. denied*, 493 U.S. 969 (1989).

he was unable to find an available federal judicial officer.[281] State officers arrested the defendants after they found contraband during the search of defendants' room, and the defendants remained in state custody. Because the time spent in state custody was exclusively the result of the federal agent's action, the defendants were entitled to credit against their eventual federal sentence for the time spent in pretrial detention.

The Fifth and Tenth Circuits have held that any credit for official detention is applied only to a term of imprisonment, not to a term of probation.[282]

The Second Circuit held that incarceration in civil contempt is not credited to the defendant's subsequent term for criminal contempt.[283]

---

281. *Id.* at 1507.
282. United States v. Dowling, 962 F.2d 390, 393 (5th Cir. 1992); United States v. Temple, 918 F.2d 134, 136 (10th Cir. 1990).
283. Ochoa v. United States, 819 F.2d 366, 369–72 (2d Cir. 1987).

For Further Reference

Bruce D. Pringle, *Bail and Detention in Federal Criminal Proceedings*, 22 Colo. Law. 913 (May 1993)

Jack L. Weinberg, Federal Bail and Detention Handbook (Practising Law Institute 1998)

11 Charles Alan Wright, Arthur R. Miller & Edward H. Cooper, Federal Practice and Procedure §§ 761–779 (3d ed. 1998)

Jonathan W. Feldman, The Fundamentals of Criminal Pretrial in the Federal Courts (2006) (forthcoming) (videotape and outline available at http://cwn.fjc.dcn/library/fjc_catalog.nsf)

The Crime Victims' Rights Act of 2004 and the Federal Courts (Federal Judicial Center, Oct. 24, 2005) (available at http://www.fjc.gov/library/fjc_catalog.nsf and http://cwn.fjc.gov)

Blank pages inserted to preserve pagination when printing double-sided copies.

Appendix A

The Bail Reform Act of 1984, 18 U.S.C. §§ 3141–3150, 3156

§ 3141. Release and detention authority generally

(a) Pending trial.—A judicial officer authorized to order the arrest of a person under section 3041 of this title before whom an arrested person is brought shall order that such person be released or detained, pending judicial proceedings, under this chapter.

(b) Pending sentence or appeal.—A judicial officer of a court of original jurisdiction over an offense, or a judicial officer of a Federal appellate court, shall order that, pending imposition or execution of sentence, or pending appeal of conviction or sentence, a person be released or detained under this chapter.

§ 3142. Release or detention of a defendant pending trial

(a) In general.—Upon the appearance before a judicial officer of a person charged with an offense, the judicial officer shall issue an order that, pending trial, the person be—

(1) released on personal recognizance or upon execution of an unsecured appearance bond, under subsection (b) of this section;

(2) released on a condition or combination of conditions under subsection (c) of this section;

(3) temporarily detained to permit revocation of conditional release, deportation, or exclusion under subsection (d) of this section; or

(4) detained under subsection (e) of this section.

(b) Release on personal recognizance or unsecured appearance bond.—The judicial officer shall order the pretrial release of the person on personal recognizance, or upon execution of an unsecured appearance bond in an amount specified by the court, subject to the condition that the person not commit a Federal, State, or local crime during the period of release, unless the judicial officer determines that such release will not reasonably assure the appearance of the person as required or will endanger the safety of any other person or the community.

(c) Release on conditions.—(1) If the judicial officer determines that the release described in subsection (b) of this section will not reasonably assure the appearance of the person as required or will endanger the safety of any other person or the community, such judicial officer shall order the pretrial release of the person—

    (A) subject to the condition that the person not commit a Federal, State, or local crime during the period of release; and

    (B) subject to the least restrictive further condition, or combination of conditions, that such judicial officer determines will reasonably assure the appearance of the person as required and the safety of any other person and the community, which may include the condition that the person—

        (i) remain in the custody of a designated person, who agrees to assume supervision and to report any violation of a release condition to the court, if the designated person is able reasonably to assure the judicial officer that the person will appear as required and will not pose a danger to the safety of any other person or the community;

        (ii) maintain employment, or, if unemployed, actively seek employment;

        (iii) maintain or commence an educational program;

        (iv) abide by specified restrictions on personal associations, place of abode, or travel;

        (v) avoid all contact with an alleged victim of the crime and with a potential witness who may testify concerning the offense;

        (vi) report on a regular basis to a designated law enforcement agency, pretrial services agency, or other agency;

        (vii) comply with a specified curfew;

        (viii) refrain from possessing a firearm, destructive device, or other dangerous weapon;

(ix) refrain from excessive use of alcohol, or any use of a narcotic drug or other controlled substance, as defined in section 102 of the Controlled Substances Act (21 U.S.C. § 802), without a prescription by a licensed medical practitioner;

(x) undergo available medical, psychological, or psychiatric treatment, including treatment for drug or alcohol dependency, and remain in a specified institution if required for that purpose;

(xi) execute an agreement to forfeit upon failing to appear as required, property of a sufficient unencumbered value, including money, as is reasonably necessary to assure the appearance of the person as required, and shall provide the court with proof of ownership and the value of the property along with information regarding existing encumbrances as the judicial officer may require;

(xii) execute a bail bond with solvent sureties; who will execute an agreement to forfeit in such amount as is reasonably necessary to assure appearance of the person as required and shall provide the court with information regarding the value of the assets and liabilities of the surety if other than an approved surety and the nature and extent of encumbrances against the surety's property; such surety shall have a net worth which shall have sufficient unencumbered value to pay the amount of the bail bond;

(xiii) return to custody for specified hours following release for employment, schooling, or other limited purposes; and

(xiv) satisfy any other condition that is reasonably necessary to assure the appearance of the person as required and to assure the safety of any other person and the community.

(2) The judicial officer may not impose a financial condition that results in the pretrial detention of the person.

(3) The judicial officer may at any time amend the order to impose additional or different conditions of release.

(d) Temporary detention to permit revocation of conditional release, deportation, or exclusion.—If the judicial officer determines that—

(1) such person—

(A) is, and was at the time the offense was committed, on—
  (i) release pending trial for a felony under Federal, State, or local law;
  (ii) release pending imposition or execution of sentence, appeal of sentence or conviction, or completion of sentence, for any offense under Federal, State, or local law; or
  (iii) probation or parole for any offense under Federal, State, or local law; or
(B) is not a citizen of the United States or lawfully admitted for permanent residence, as defined in section 101(a)(20) of the Immigration and Nationality Act (8 U.S.C. § 1101(a)(20)); and
(2) the person may flee or pose a danger to any other person or the community; such judicial officer shall order the detention of the person, for a period of not more than ten days, excluding Saturdays, Sundays, and holidays, and direct the attorney for the Government to notify the appropriate court, probation or parole official, or State or local law enforcement official, or the appropriate official of the Immigration and Naturalization Service. If the official fails or declines to take the person into custody during that period, the person shall be treated in accordance with the other provisions of this section, notwithstanding the applicability of other provisions of law governing release pending trial or deportation or exclusion proceedings. If temporary detention is sought under paragraph (1)(B) of this subsection, the person has the burden of proving to the court such person's United States citizenship or lawful admission for permanent residence.

(e) Detention.—If, after a hearing pursuant to the provisions of subsection (f) of this section, the judicial officer finds that no condition or combination of conditions will reasonably assure the appearance of the person as required and the safety of any other person and the community, such judicial officer shall order the detention of the person before trial. In a case described in subsection (f)(1) of this section, a rebuttable presumption arises that no condition or combination of conditions will reasonably assure the safety of any other person and the community if such judicial officer finds that—

(1) the person has been convicted of a Federal offense that is described in subsection (f)(1) of this section, or of a State or local offense that would have been an offense described in subsection (f)(1) of this section if a circumstance giving rise to Federal jurisdiction had existed;

(2) the offense described in paragraph (1) of this subsection was committed while the person was on release pending trial for a Federal, State, or local offense; and

(3) a period of not more than five years has elapsed since the date of conviction, or the release of the person from imprisonment, for the offense described in paragraph (1) of this subsection, whichever is later.

Subject to rebuttal by the person, it shall be presumed that no condition or combination of conditions will reasonably assure the appearance of the person as required and the safety of the community if the judicial officer finds that there is probable cause to believe that the person committed an offense for which a maximum term of imprisonment of ten years or more is prescribed in the Controlled Substances Act (21 U.S.C. § 801 et seq.), the Controlled Substances Import and Export Act (21 U.S.C. § 951 et seq.), the Maritime Drug Law Enforcement Act (46 U.S.C. App. 1901 et seq.), or an offense under section 924(c), 956(a), or 2332b of this title, or an offense listed in section 2332b(g)(5)(B) of title 18, the United States Code, for which the maximum term of imprisonment of ten years or more is prescribed or an offense involving a minor victim under section 1201, 1591, 2241, 2242, 2244(a)(1), 2245, 2251, 2251A, 2252(a)(1), 2252(a)(2), 2252(a)(3), 2252A(a)(1), 2252A(a)(2), 2252A(a)(3), 2252A(a)(4), 2260, 2421, 2422, 2423, or 2425 of this title.

(f) Detention hearing.—The judicial officer shall hold a hearing to determine whether any condition or combination of conditions set forth in subsection (c) of this section will reasonably assure the appearance of the person as required and the safety of any other person and the community—

(1) upon motion of the attorney for the Government, in a case that involves—

(A) a crime of violence, or an offense listed in section 2332b(g)(5)(B) for which the maximum term of imprisonment of ten years or more is prescribed;
(B) an offense for which the maximum sentence is life imprisonment or death;
(C) an offense for which a maximum term of imprisonment of ten years or more is prescribed in the Controlled Substances Act (21 U.S.C. § 801 et seq.), the Controlled Substances Import and Export Act (21 U.S.C. § 951 et seq.), or the Maritime Drug Law Enforcement Act (46 U.S.C. App. 1901 et seq.); or
(D) any felony if the person has been convicted of two or more offenses described in subparagraphs (A) through (C) of this paragraph, or two or more State or local offenses that would have been offenses described in subparagraphs (A) through (C) of this paragraph if a circumstance giving rise to Federal jurisdiction had existed, or a combination of such offenses; or
(2) upon motion of the attorney for the Government or upon the judicial officer's own motion, in a case that involves—
(A) a serious risk that the person will flee; or
(B) a serious risk that the person will obstruct or attempt to obstruct justice, or threaten, injure, or intimidate, or attempt to threaten, injure, or intimidate, a prospective witness or juror.

The hearing shall be held immediately upon the person's first appearance before the judicial officer unless that person, or the attorney for the Government, seeks a continuance. Except for good cause, a continuance on motion of the person may not exceed five days (not including any intermediate Saturday, Sunday, or legal holiday), and a continuance on motion of the attorney for the Government may not exceed three days (not including any intermediate Saturday, Sunday, or legal holiday). During a continuance, the person shall be detained, and the judicial officer, on motion of the attorney for the Government or sua sponte, may order that, while in custody, a person who appears to be a narcotics addict receive a medical examination to determine whether such person is an addict. At the hearing, such person has the right to be represented by counsel, and, if financially unable to obtain adequate representation, to have counsel appointed. The person shall be afforded an opportunity to testify, to present witnesses, to cross-examine witnesses who appear at the hearing, and to present information by proffer or otherwise. The rules concerning admissibility of evidence in criminal trials do not apply to the presentation and consideration of information at the hearing. The facts the judicial officer uses to support a finding pursuant to subsection (e) that no condition or combination of conditions will reasonably assure the safety of any other person and the community shall be supported by clear and convincing evidence. The person may be detained pending completion of the hearing. The hearing may be reopened before or after a determination by the judicial officer, at any time before trial if the judicial officer finds that information exists that was not known to the movant at the time of the hearing and that has a material bearing on the issue whether there are conditions of release that will reasonably assure the appearance of the person as required and the safety of any other person and the community.

(g) Factors to be considered.—The judicial officer shall, in determining whether there are conditions of release that will reasonably assure the appearance of the person as required and the safety of any other person and the community, take into account the available information concerning—

(1) the nature and circumstances of the offense charged, including whether the offense is a crime of violence, or an offense listed in section 2332b(g)(5)(B) for which a maximum term of imprisonment of nineteen years or more is prescribed or involves a narcotic drug;

(2) the weight of the evidence against the person;

(3) the history and characteristics of the person, including—

(A) the person's character, physical and mental condition, family ties, employment, financial resources, length of residence in the community, community ties, past conduct, history relating to drug or alcohol abuse, criminal history, and record concerning appearance at court proceedings; and

(B) whether, at the time of the current offense or arrest, the person was on probation, on parole, or on other release pending trial, sentencing, appeal, or completion of sentence for an offense under Federal, State, or local law; and

(4) the nature and seriousness of the danger to any person or the community that would be posed by the person's release. In considering the conditions of release described in subsection (c)(1)(B)(xi) or (c)(1)(B)(xii) of this section, the judicial officer may upon his own motion, or shall upon the motion of the Government, conduct an inquiry into the source of the property to be designated for potential forfeiture or offered as collateral to secure a bond, and shall decline to accept the designation, or the use as collateral, of property that, because of its source, will not reasonably assure the appearance of the person as required.

(h) Contents of release order.—In a release order issued under subsection (b) or (c) of this section, the judicial officer shall—

(1) include a written statement that sets forth all the conditions to which the release is subject, in a manner sufficiently clear and specific to serve as a guide for the person's conduct; and

(2) advise the person of—

(A) the penalties for violating a condition of release, including the penalties for committing an offense while on pretrial release;

(B) the consequences of violating a condition of release, including the immediate issuance of a warrant for the person's arrest; and

(C) sections 1503 of this title (relating to intimidation of witnesses, jurors, and officers of the court), 1510 (relating to obstruction of criminal investigations), 1512 (tampering with a witness, victim, or an informant), and 1513 (retaliating against a witness, victim, or an informant).

(i) Contents of detention order.—In a detention order issued under subsection (e) of this section, the judicial officer shall—

(1) include written findings of fact and a written statement of the reasons for the detention;

(2) direct that the person be committed to the custody of the Attorney General for confinement in a corrections facility separate, to the extent practicable, from persons awaiting or serving sentences or being held in custody pending appeal;

(3) direct that the person be afforded reasonable opportunity for private consultation with counsel; and

(4) direct that, on order of a court of the United States or on request of an attorney for the Government, the person in charge of the corrections facility in which the person is confined deliver the person to a United States marshal for the purpose of an appearance in connection with a court proceeding.

The judicial officer may, by subsequent order, permit the temporary release of the person, in the custody of a United States marshal or another appropriate person, to the extent that the judicial officer determines such release to be necessary for preparation of the person's defense or for another compelling reason.

(j) Presumption of innocence.—Nothing in this section shall be construed as modifying or limiting the presumption of innocence.

§ 3143. Release or detention of a defendant pending sentence or appeal

(a) Release or detention pending sentence.—(1) Except as provided in paragraph (2), the judicial officer shall order that a person who has been found guilty of an offense and who is awaiting imposition or execution of sentence, other than a person for whom the applicable guideline promulgated pursuant to 28 U.S.C. § 994 does not recommend a term of imprisonment, be detained, unless the judicial officer finds by clear and convincing evidence that the person is not likely to flee or pose a danger to the safety of any other person or the community if released under section 3142(b) or (c). If the judicial officer makes such a finding, such judicial officer shall order the release of the person in accordance with section 3142(b) or (c).

(2) The judicial officer shall order that a person who has been found guilty of an offense in a case described in subparagraph (A), (B), or (C) of subsection (f)(1) of section 3142 and is awaiting imposition or execution of sentence be detained unless—

(A)(i) the judicial officer finds there is a substantial likelihood that a motion for acquittal or new trial will be granted; or

(ii) an attorney for the Government has recommended that no sentence of imprisonment be imposed on the person; and

(B) the judicial officer finds by clear and convincing evidence that the person is not likely to flee or pose a danger to any other person or the community.

(b) Release or detention pending appeal by the defendant.—(1) Except as provided in paragraph (2), the judicial officer shall order that a person who has been found guilty of an offense and sentenced to a term of imprisonment, and who has filed an appeal or a petition for a writ of certiorari, be detained, unless the judicial officer finds—

> (A) by clear and convincing evidence that the person is not likely to flee or pose a danger to the safety of any other person or the community if released under section 3142(b) or (c) of this title; and
>
> (B) that the appeal is not for the purpose of delay and raises a substantial question of law or fact likely to result in—
>
>> (i) reversal,
>> (ii) an order for a new trial,
>> (iii) a sentence that does not include a term of imprisonment, or
>> (iv) a reduced sentence to a term of imprisonment less than the total of the time already served plus the expected duration of the appeal process.

If the judicial officer makes such findings, such judicial officer shall order the release of the person in accordance with section 3142(b) or (c) of this title, except that in the circumstance described in subparagraph (b)(iv) of this paragraph, the judicial officer shall order the detention terminated at the expiration of the likely reduced sentence.

> (2) The judicial officer shall order that a person who has been found guilty of an offense in a case described in subparagraph (A), (B), or (C) of subsection (f)(1) of section 3142 and sentenced to a term of imprisonment, and who has filed an appeal or a petition for a writ of certiorari, be detained.

(c) Release or detention pending appeal by the government.—The judicial officer shall treat a defendant in a case in which an appeal has been taken by the United States under section 3731 of this title, in accordance with section 3142 of this title, unless the defendant is otherwise subject to a release or detention order. Except as provided in subsection (b) of this section, the judicial officer, in a case in which an appeal has been taken by the United States under section 3742, shall—

(1) if the person has been sentenced to a term of imprisonment, order that person detained; and

(2) in any other circumstance, release or detain the person under section 3142.

§ 3144. Release or detention of a material witness

If it appears from an affidavit filed by a party that the testimony of a person is material in a criminal proceeding, and if it is shown that it may become impracticable to secure the presence of the person by subpoena, a judicial officer may order the arrest of the person and treat the person in accordance with the provisions of section 3142 of this title. No material witness may be detained because of inability to comply with any condition of release if the testimony of such witness can adequately be secured by deposition, and if further detention is not necessary to prevent a failure of justice. Release of a material witness may be delayed for a reasonable period of time until the deposition of the witness can be taken pursuant to the Federal Rules of Criminal Procedure.

§ 3145. Review and appeal of a release or detention order

(a) Review of a release order.—If a person is ordered released by a magistrate, or by a person other than a judge of a court having original jurisdiction over the offense and other than a Federal appellate court—

(1) the attorney for the Government may file, with the court having original jurisdiction over the offense, a motion for revocation of the order or amendment of the conditions of release; and

(2) the person may file, with the court having original jurisdiction over the offense, a motion for amendment of the conditions of release.

The motion shall be determined promptly.

(b) Review of a detention order.—If a person is ordered detained by a magistrate, or by a person other than a judge of a court having original jurisdiction over the offense and other than a Federal appellate court, the person may file, with the court having original jurisdiction over the offense, a motion for revocation or amendment of the order. The motion shall be determined promptly.

(c) Appeal from a release or detention order.—An appeal from a release or detention order, or from a decision denying revocation or amendment of such an order, is governed by the provisions of section 1291 of title 28 and section 3731 of this title. The appeal shall be determined promptly. A person subject to detention pursuant to section 3143(a)(2) or (b)(2), and who meets the conditions of release set forth in section 3143(a)(1) or (b)(1), may be ordered released, under appropriate conditions, by the judicial officer, if it is clearly shown that there are exceptional reasons why such person's detention would not be appropriate.

§ 3146. Penalty for failure to appear

(a) Offense.—Whoever, having been released under this chapter knowingly—

(1) fails to appear before a court as required by the conditions of release; or

(2) fails to surrender for service of sentence pursuant to a court order; shall be punished as provided in subsection (b) of this section.

(b) Punishment.—(1) The punishment for an offense under this section is—

(A) if the person was released in connection with a charge of, or while awaiting sentence, surrender for service of sentence, or appeal or certiorari after conviction for—

(i) an offense punishable by death, life imprisonment, or imprisonment for a term of 15 years or more, a fine under this title or imprisonment for not more than ten years, or both;

(ii) an offense punishable by imprisonment for a term of five years or more, a fine under this title or imprisonment for not more than five years, or both;

(iii) any other felony, a fine under this title or imprisonment for not more than two years, or both; or

(iv) a misdemeanor, a fine under this title or imprisonment for not more than one year, or both; and

(B) if the person was released for appearance as a material witness, a fine under this chapter or imprisonment for not more than one year, or both.

(2) A term of imprisonment imposed under this section shall be consecutive to the sentence of imprisonment for any other offense.

(c) Affirmative defense.—It is an affirmative defense to a prosecution under this section that uncontrollable circumstances prevented the person from appearing or surrendering, and that the person did not contribute to the creation of such circumstances in reckless disregard of the requirement to appear or surrender, and that the person appeared or surrendered as soon as such circumstances ceased to exist.

(d) Declaration of forfeiture.—If a person fails to appear before a court as required, and the person executed an appearance bond pursuant to section 3142(b) of this title or is subject to the release condition set forth in clause (xi) or (xii) of section 3142(c)(1)(B) of this title, the judicial officer may, regardless of whether the person has been charged with an offense under this section, declare any property designated pursuant to that section to be forfeited to the United States.

§ 3147. Penalty for an offense committed while on release

A person convicted of an offense committed while released under this chapter shall be sentenced, in addition to the sentence prescribed for the offense to—

(1) a term of imprisonment of not more than ten years if the offense is a felony; or

(2) a term of imprisonment of not more than one year if the offense is a misdemeanor.

A term of imprisonment imposed under this section shall be consecutive to any other sentence of imprisonment.

Section applicable to offenses committed prior to November 1, 1987

This section as in effect prior to amendment by Pub. L. No. 98-473, read as follows:

§ 3147. Penalty for an offense committed while on release

A person convicted of an offense committed while released under this chapter shall be sentenced, in addition to the sentence prescribed for the offense, to—
   (1) a term of imprisonment of not less than two years and not more than ten years if the offense is a felony; or
   (2) a term of imprisonment of not less than ninety days and not more than one year if the offense is a misdemeanor.

A term of imprisonment imposed under this section shall be consecutive to any other sentence of imprisonment.

For applicability of sentencing provisions to offenses, see Effective Date and Savings Provisions, etc., note, section 235 of Pub. L. No. 98-473, as amended, set out under section 3551 of this title.

§ 3148. Sanctions for violation of a release condition

(a) Available sanctions.—A person who has been released under section 3142 of this title, and who has violated a condition of his release, is subject to a revocation of release, an order of detention, and a prosecution for contempt of court.

(b) Revocation of release.—The attorney for the Government may initiate a proceeding for revocation of an order of release by filing a motion with the district court. A judicial officer may issue a warrant for the arrest of a person charged with violating a condition of release, and the person shall be brought before a judicial officer in the district in which such person's arrest was ordered for a proceeding in accordance with this section. To the extent practicable, a person charged with violating the condition of release that such person not commit a Federal, State, or local crime during the period of release, shall be brought before the judicial officer who ordered the release and whose order is alleged to have been violated. The judicial officer shall enter an order of revocation and detention if, after a hearing, the judicial officer—
   (1) finds that there is—
      (A) probable cause to believe that the person has committed a Federal, State, or local crime while on release; or

(B) clear and convincing evidence that the person has violated any other condition of release; and

(2) finds that—

(A) based on the factors set forth in section 3142(g) of this title, there is no condition or combination of conditions of release that will assure that the person will not flee or pose a danger to the safety of any other person or the community; or

(B) the person is unlikely to abide by any condition or combination of conditions of release.

If there is probable cause to believe that, while on release, the person committed a Federal, State, or local felony, a rebuttable presumption arises that no condition or combination of conditions will assure that the person will not pose a danger to the safety of any other person or the community. If the judicial officer finds that there are conditions of release that will assure that the person will not flee or pose a danger to the safety of any other person or the community, and that the person will abide by such conditions, the judicial officer shall treat the person in accordance with the provisions of section 3142 of this title and may amend the conditions of release accordingly.

(c) Prosecution for contempt.—The judicial officer may commence a prosecution for contempt, under section 401 of this title, if the person has violated a condition of release.

§ 3149. Surrender of an offender by a surety

A person charged with an offense, who is released upon the execution of an appearance bond with a surety, may be arrested by the surety, and if so arrested, shall be delivered promptly to a United States marshal and brought before a judicial officer. The judicial officer shall determine in accordance with the provisions of section 3148(b) whether to revoke the release of the person, and may absolve the surety of responsibility to pay all or part of the bond in accordance with the provisions of Rule 46 of the Federal Rules of Criminal Procedure. The person so committed shall be held in official detention until released pursuant to this chapter or another provision of law.

§ 3150. Applicability to a case removed from a State court

The provisions of this chapter apply to a criminal case removed to a Federal court from a State court.

§ 3156. Definitions

(a) As used in sections 3141–3150 of this chapter—

(1) the term "judicial officer" means, unless otherwise indicated, any person or court authorized pursuant to section 3041 of this title, or the Federal Rules of Criminal Procedure, to detain or release a person before trial or sentencing or pending appeal in a court of the United States, and any judge of the Superior Court of the District of Columbia;

(2) the term "offense" means any criminal offense, other than an offense triable by court-martial, military commission, provost court, or other military tribunal, which is in violation of an Act of Congress and is triable in any court established by Act of Congress;

(3) the term "felony" means an offense punishable by a maximum term of imprisonment of more than one year; and

(4) the term "crime of violence" means—

(A) an offense that has as an element of the offense the use, attempted use, or threatened use of physical force against the person or property of another; or

(B) any other offense that is a felony and that, by its nature, involves a substantial risk that physical force against the person or property of another may be used in the course of committing the offense.

Appendix B

The Sentencing Reform Act of 1984
Selected Provision: 18 U.S.C. § 3585

§ 3585. Calculation of a term of imprisonment

(a) Commencement of sentence.—A sentence to a term of imprisonment commences on the date the defendant is received in custody awaiting transportation to, or arrives voluntarily to commence service of sentence at, the official detention facility at which the sentence is to be served.

(b) Credit for prior custody.—A defendant shall be given credit toward the service of a term of imprisonment for any time he has spent in official detention prior to the date the sentence commences—

    (1) as a result of the offense for which the sentence was imposed; or
    (2) as a result of any other charge for which the defendant was arrested after the commission of the offense for which the sentence was imposed; that has not been credited against another sentence.

Blank pages inserted to preserve pagination when printing double-sided copies.

Table of Cases

Apprendi v. New Jersey, 530 U.S. 466 (2000), n.261
Barcal v. United States, 510 F.2d 814 (1993), n.242
Bell v. Wolfish, 441 U.S. 520 (1979), n.28
Cherek v. United States, 767 F.2d 335 (7th Cir. 1985), n.230
Class Action Application for Habeas Corpus on Behalf of All Material Witnesses in the Western District of Texas, *In re*, 612 F. Supp. 940 (W.D. Tex. 1985), n.248
Cohen v. United States, 492 U.S. 906 (1989), nn.259
Cucciniello v. Keller, 137 F.3d 721 (2d Cir. 1998), nn.278–79
Fassler v. United States, 858 F.2d 1016 (5th Cir. 1988), n.98
Kenna v. United States District Court for the Central District of California, 435 F.3d 1011 (9th Cir. 2006), n.150
Montgomery County Fire Board v. Fisher, 454 A.2d 394 (1983), n.94
Morison v. United States, 486 U.S. 1306 (1987), n.222
Murphy v. Hunt, 455 U.S. 478 (1982), n.167
Ochoa v. United States, 819 F.2d 366 (2d Cir. 1987), n.283
Peralta v. United States, 522 U.S. 900 (1997), n.259
Reno v. Koray, 515 U.S. 50 (1995), nn.276–77
Rodriguez v. United States, 480 U.S. 522 (1987), n.251
United States v. Abuhamra, 389 F.3d 309 (2d Cir. 2004), n.129
United States v. Accetturo, 783 F.2d 382 (3d Cir. 1986), nn.38, 119, 120, 125, 126, 130, 139, 157
United States v. Acevedo-Ramos, 755 F.2d 203 (1st Cir. 1985), nn.37, 118, 120, 132
United States v. Affleck, 765 F.2d 944 (10th Cir. 1985), nn.223, 225, 234, 240
United States v. Aitken, 898 F.2d 104 (9th Cir. 1990), n.40
United States v. Al-Azzawy, 768 F.2d 1141 (9th Cir. 1985), nn.63, 73, 77, 109
United States v. Alatishe, 768 F.2d 364 (D.C. Cir. 1985), nn.78, 90, 91, 106–09
United States v. Angiulo, 755 F.2d 969 (1st Cir. 1985), nn.133, 134
United States v. Apker, 964 F.2d 742 (8th Cir. 1992), n.133
United States v. Araneda, 899 F.2d 368 (5th Cir. 1990), nn.76, 199
United States v. Aron, 904 F.2d 221 (5th Cir. 1990), nn.171, 175, 199

United States v. Ashman, 964 F.2d 596 (7th Cir. 1992), n.242
United States v. Awadallah, 349 F.3d 42 (2d Cir. 2003), n.249
United States v. Barker, 876 F.2d 475 (5th Cir. 1989), nn.193, 199
United States v. Bayko, 774 F.2d 516 (1st Cir. 1985), nn.234, 240
United States v. Becerra-Cobo, 790 F.2d 427 (5th Cir. 1986), nn.107, 108, 109
United States v. Benson, 134 F.3d 787 (6th Cir. 1998), n.256
United States v. Berrios-Berrios, 791 F.2d 246 (2d Cir. 1986), nn.134, 135, 142, 197
United States v. Bilanzich, 771 F.2d 292 (7th Cir. 1985), nn.223, 241, 242
United States v. Blasini-Lluberas, 144 F.3d 881 (1st Cir. 1998), n.17
United States v. Bloomer, 967 F.2d 761 (2d Cir. 1992), n.214
United States v. Bolding, 972 F.2d 184 (8th Cir. 1992), n.270
United States v. Booker, 543 U.S. 220 (2005), nn.205, 232, 263
United States v. Booker, 375 F.3d 508 (7th Cir. 2004), n.232
United States v. Bowers, 432 F.3d 518 (3d Cir. 2005), nn.54, 55
United States v. Brown, 870 F.2d 1354 (7th Cir. 1989), n.5
United States v. Byrd, 969 F.2d 106 (5th Cir. 1992), nn.48, 49
United States v. Cantu, 935 F.2d 950 (8th Cir. 1991), nn.17, 204
United States v. Carbone, 793 F.2d 559 (3d Cir. 1986), n.97
United States v. Cardenas, 784 F.2d 937 (9th Cir. 1986), nn.118, 123, 125, 132
United States v. Carey, 943 F.2d 44 (11th Cir. 1991), n.270
United States v. Carr, 947 F.2d 1239 (5th Cir. 1992), nn.86, 209
United States v. Castiello, 878 F.2d 554 (1st Cir. 1989), n.233
United States v. Chappell, 854 F.2d 190 (7th Cir. 1988), n.271
United States v. Chimurenga, 760 F.2d 400 (2d Cir. 1985), nn.51, 89, 90, 196
United States v. Ciccone, 312 F.3d 535 (2d Cir. 2002), n.52
United States v. Cisneros, 328 F.3d 610 (10th Cir. 2003), nn.182, 183
United States v. Clark, 865 F.2d 1433 (4th Cir. 1989), nn.79, 184, 194, 198
United States v. Coleman, 777 F.2d 888 (3d Cir. 1985), n.17
United States v. Colombo, 777 F.2d 96 (2d Cir. 1985), n.35
United States v. Contreras, 776 F.2d 51 (2d Cir. 1985), n.88
United States v. Cook, 880 F.2d 1158 (10th Cir. 1989), nn.171, 173
United States v. Coonan, 826 F.2d 1180 (2d Cir. 1987), nn.76, 80, 81
United States v. Cooper, 827 F.2d 991 (4th Cir. 1987), n.258
United States v. Crabtree, 754 F.2d 1200 (5th Cir. 1985), n.223
United States v. Daniels, 772 F.2d 382 (7th Cir. 1985), nn.91, 97

United States v. Davis, 845 F.2d 412 (2d Cir. 1988), nn.18, 176
United States v. Dean, 927 F.2d 605 (6th Cir. 1991), n.102
United States v. Degenhardt, 405 F. Supp.2d 1341 (D. Utah 2005), n.150
United States v. Delanoy, 867 F. Supp. 114 (N.D.N.Y. 1994), n.225
United States v. Delker, 757 F.2d 1390 (3d Cir. 1985), nn.60, 114, 118, 121, 125, 184, 185, 186, 203
United States v. Diaz, 777 F.2d 1236 (7th Cir. 1985), n.90
United States v. DiCaro, 852 F.2d 259 (7th Cir. 1988), n.258
United States v. Dillard, 214 F.3d 88 (2d Cir. 2000), n.53
United States v. Dillon, 938 F.2d 1412 (1st Cir. 1991), nn.93, 155
United States v. DiPasquale, 864 F.2d 271 (3d Cir. 1988), nn.259, 260
United States v. DiSomma, 951 F.2d 494 (2d Cir. 1991), nn.220, 244, 245
United States v. Dominguez, 783 F.2d 702 (7th Cir. 1986), nn.71, 88, 90, 93, 96, 97
United States v. Dowling, 962 F.2d 390 (5th Cir. 1992), n.282
United States v. Eaken, 995 F.2d 740 (7th Cir. 1993), n.234
United States v. El-Edwy, 272 F.3d 149 (2d Cir. 2001), n.182
United States v. El-Gabrowny, 35 F.3d 63 (2d Cir. 1994), n.162
United States v. El-Hage, 213 F.3d 74 (2d Cir. 2000), nn.157, 162
United States v. Ellis, 241 F.3d 1096 (9th Cir. 2001), n.262
United States v. Evans, 62 F.3d 1233 (9th Cir. 1995), nn.182, 183
United States v. Feldhacker, 849 F.2d 293 (8th Cir. 1988), n.260
United States v. Fernandez-Alfonso, 813 F.2d 1571 (9th Cir. 1987), n.191
United States v. Ferranti, 66 F.3d 540 (2d Cir. 1995), n.196
United States v. Fitzgerald, 435 F.3d 484 (4th Cir. 2006), nn.256, 257
United States v. Fortna, 769 F.2d 243 (5th Cir. 1985), nn.23, 59, 78, 90, 118, 186
United States v. Frazier, 772 F.2d 1451 (9th Cir. 1985), n.5
United States v. French, 900 F.2d 1300 (8th Cir. 1990), n.5
United States v. Friedman, 837 F.2d 48 (2d Cir. 1988), nn.44, 48
United States v. Galanis, 695 F. Supp. 1565 (S.D.N.Y. 1988), n.225
United States v. Galliano, 977 F.2d 1350 (9th Cir. 1992), nn.252–53
United States v. Gaviria, 828 F.2d 667 (11th Cir. 1987), n.123
United States v. Gebro, 948 F.2d 1118 (9th Cir. 1991), nn.34, 115
United States v. Gelfuso, 838 F.2d 358 (9th Cir. 1988), nn.157, 164
United States v. Giancola, 754 F.2d 898 (11th Cir. 1985), nn.223, 234, 240
United States v. Gigante, 85 F.3d 83 (2d Cir. 1996), n.178
United States v. Gillon, 348 F.3d 755 (8th Cir. 2003), n.262

United States v. Gonzales, 852 F.2d 1214 (9th Cir. 1988), n.192
United States v. Gonzales Claudio, 806 F.2d 334 (2d Cir. 1986), n.161
United States v. Goosens, 84 F.3d 697 (4th Cir. 1996), n.5
United States v. Gotti, 794 F.2d 773 (2d Cir. 1986), nn.171, 175
United States v. Graham, 257 F.3d. 143 (2d Cir. 2001), n.128
United States v. Handy, 761 F.2d 1279 (9th Cir. 1985), nn.223, 235
United States v. Hare, 873 F.2d 796 (5th Cir. 1989), nn.35, 90, 93, 96, 155, 157, 165
United States v. Harris, 942 F.2d 1125 (7th Cir. 1991), n.228
United States v. Harris, 876 F.2d 1502 (11th Cir. 1989), nn.280–81
United States v. Hazime, 762 F.2d 34 (6th Cir. 1985), nn.88, 204
United States v. Herrera-Soto, 961 F.2d 645 (7th Cir. 1992), nn.220, 244
United States v. Himler, 797 F.2d 156 (3d Cir. 1986), nn.43, 48
United States v. Hinote, 789 F.2d 1490 (11th Cir. 1986), n.85
United States v. Holloway, 781 F.2d 124 (8th Cir. 1984), n.58
United States v. Holzer, 848 F.2d 822 (7th Cir. 1988), n.216
United States v. Hurtado, 779 F.2d 1467 (11th Cir. 1985), nn.17, 73, 74, 77, 88, 90, 127, 138, 141, 204
United States v. Infelise, 934 F.2d 103 (7th Cir. 1991), nn.24, 157, 163
United States v. Ingraham, 832 F.2d 229 (1st Cir. 1987), n.103
United States v. Jackson, 845 F.2d 1262 (5th Cir. 1988), nn.88, 199
United States v. Jackson, 823 F.2d 4 (2d Cir. 1987), n.40
United States v. Jackson, 891 F.2d 1151 (5th Cir. 1989), n.260
United States v. Jessup, 757 F.2d 378 (1st Cir. 1985), nn.11, 13, 84, 90, 92, 94, 100
United States v. Johnson, 446 F.3d 272 (2d Cir. 2006), n.8
United States v. Johnson, 399 F.3d 1297 (11th Cir. 2005), n.54
United States v. Jones, 979 F.2d 804, 806 (10th Cir. 1992), n.209
United States v. Kelly, 790 F.2d 130 (D.C. Cir. 1986), n.231
United States v. Kentz, 251 F.3d 835 (9th Cir. 2001), nn.259, 262
United States v. Kills Enemy, 3 F.3d 1201 (8th Cir. 1993), n.6
United States v. King, 849 F.2d 485 (11th Cir. 1988), nn.23, 40, 88, 184, 187
United States v. King, 818 F.2d 112 (1st Cir. 1987), nn.76, 81
United States v. Koenig, 912 F.2d 1190 (9th Cir. 1990), nn.184, 185, 186
United States v. Krilich, 178 F.3d 859 (7th Cir. 1999), n.232
United States v. LaFontaine, 210 F.3d 125 (2d Cir. 2000), n.177
United States v. Lagiglio, 384 F.3d 925 (7th Cir. 2004), n.232
United States v. Lane, 252 F.3d 905 (7th Cir. 2001), n.54

United States v. Lea, 360 F.3d 401 (2d Cir. 2004), n.246
United States v. Lee, 783 F.2d 92 (7th Cir. 1986), nn.107, 110
United States v. Leon, 766 F.2d 77 (2d Cir. 1985), nn.41, 184, 185
United States v. Lewis, 991 F.2d 322 (6th Cir. 1993), n.259
United States v. Lippold, 175 F. Supp. 2d 537 (S.D.N.Y. 2001), n.246
United States v. London-Villa, 898 F.2d 328 (2d Cir. 1990), n.212
United States v. Loya, 23 F.3d 1529 (9th Cir. 1994), n.250
United States v. Mack, 938 F.2d 678 (6th Cir. 1991), n.270
United States v. Madruga, 810 F.2d 1010 (11th Cir. 1987), n.76
United States v. Manso-Portes, 838 F.2d 889 (7th Cir. 1987), nn.207, 211, 213
United States v. Mantecon-Zayas, 949 F.2d 548 (1st Cir. 1991), nn.11, 12, 14
United States v. Marcello, 370 F. Supp. 2d 745 (N.D. Ill. 2005), n.150
United States v. Martin-Trigona, 767 F.2d 35 (2d Cir. 1985), n.137
United States v. Martinez, 890 F.2d 1088 (10th Cir. 1989), nn.265–67
United States v. Martir, 782 F.2d 1141 (2d Cir. 1986), nn.90, 93, 123
United States v. Maull, 773 F.2d 1479 (8th Cir. 1985), nn.60, 115, 184, 186
United States v. McConnell, 842 F.2d 105 (5th Cir. 1988), nn.11, 14, 40
United States v. McKethan, 602 F. Supp. 719 (D.D.C. 1985), n.174
United States v. Medina, 775 F.2d 1398 (11th Cir. 1985), nn.114, 185
United States v. Melendez-Carrion, 790 F.2d 984 (2d Cir. 1986), nn.71, 75, 140
United States v. Millan, 4 F.3d 1038 (2d Cir. 1993), nn.160, 196
United States v. Miller, 753 F.2d 19 (3d Cir. 1985), nn.223, 236–39
United States v. Molinaro, 876 F.2d 1432 (9th Cir. 1989), n.63
United States v. Moncada-Pelaez, 810 F.2d 1008 (11th Cir. 1987), n.107
United States v. Montalvo-Murillo, 495 U.S. 711 (1990), nn.62, 63, 66–70, 189, 204
United States v. Montalvo-Murillo, 713 F. Supp. 1407 (D.N.M. 1989), n.64
United States v. Montalvo-Murillo, 876 F.2d 826 (10th Cir. 1989), nn.65, 204
United States v. Montoya, 908 F.2d 450 (9th Cir. 1990), nn.223, 235
United States v. Moss, 887 F.2d 333 (1st Cir. 1989), nn.86, 87, 90
United States v. Mostrom, 11 F.3d 93 (2d Cir. 1993), n.246
United States v. Motamedi, 767 F.2d 1403 (9th Cir. 1985), n.34
United States v. Nebbia, 357 F.2d 303 (2d Cir. 1966), n.15
United States v. O'Brien, 895 F.2d 810 (1st Cir. 1990), nn.15, 202
United States v. O'Shaughnessy, 764 F.2d 1035 (5th Cir. 1985), nn.59, 63
United States v. Ojeda Rios, 846 F.2d 167 (2d Cir. 1986), nn.157, 158

United States v. Onick, 889 F.2d 1425 (5th Cir. 1989), nn.21, 258
United States v. Orena, 986 F.2d 628 (2d Cir. 1993), n.162
United States v. Orta, 760 F.2d 887 (8th Cir. 1985), nn.27, 40, 90
United States v. Pace, 955 F.2d 270 (5th Cir. 1992), nn.254–55
United States v. Palmer-Contreras, 835 F.2d 15 (1st Cir. 1987), nn.95, 190
United States v. Parker, 848 F.2d 61 (5th Cir. 1988), n.103
United States v. Parolin, 239 F.3d 922 (7th Cir. 2001), n.262
United States v. Patriarca, 948 F.2d 789 (1st Cir. 1991), nn.9, 40, 202
United States v. Patterson, 820 F.2d 1524 (9th Cir. 1987), n.260
United States v. Payden, 759 F.2d 202 (2d Cir. 1985), nn.57, 63
United States v. Peralta, 849 F.2d 625 (D.C. Cir. 1988), nn.18, 154
United States v. Perholtz, 836 F.2d 554 (D.C. Cir. 1987), n.234
United States v. Perry, 788 F.2d 100 (3d Cir. 1986), nn.41, 90, 91, 101, 131
United States v. Ploof, 851 F.2d 7 (1st Cir. 1988), n.48
United States v. Pollard, 778 F.2d 1177 (6th Cir. 1985), nn.234, 241
United States v. Portes, 786 F.2d 758 (7th Cir. 1985), nn.40, 90, 204
United States v. Powell, 761 F.2d 1227 (8th Cir. 1985), nn.223, 234, 241
United States v. Quartermaine, 913 F.2d 910 (11th Cir. 1990), nn.35, 45, 48
United States v. Quinnones, 610 F. Supp. 74 (S.D.N.Y. 1985), n.141
United States v. Ramirez, 843 F.2d 256 (7th Cir. 1988), n.23
United States v. Randall, 287 F.3d 27 (1st Cir. 2002), n.262
United States v. Randell, 761 F.2d 122 (2d Cir. 1985), nn.223, 234, 240
United States v. Reynolds, 956 F.2d 192 (9th Cir. 1992), n.42
United States v. Rodriguez, 950 F.2d 85 (2d Cir. 1991), nn.45, 48
United States v. Rogers, 371 F.3d 1225 (10th Cir. 2004), nn.53, 55
United States v. Rose, 791 F.2d 1477 (11th Cir. 1986), n.5
United States v. Rueben, 974 F.2d 580 (5th Cir. 1992), nn.96, 184
United States v. Salerno, 481 U.S. 739 (1987), nn.26, 29, 30, 156, 159
United States v. Salerno, 794 F.2d 64 (2d Cir. 1986), n.136
United States v. Samuel, 296 F.3d 1169 (D.C. Cir. 2002), n.262
United States v. Sazenski, 806 F.2d 846 (8th Cir. 1986), n.23
United States v. Scott, 450 F.3d 863 (9th Cir. 2006), n.6
United States v. Shakur, 817 F.2d 189 (2d Cir. 1987), nn.36, 104
United States v. Simmons, 912 F.2d 1215 (10th Cir. 1990), nn.265–66, 268
United States v. Singleton, 182 F.3d 7 (D.C. Cir. 1999), nn.54, 55
United States v. Smith, 793 F.2d 85 (3d Cir. 1986), nn.223, 236

United States v. Snyder, 946 F.2d 1125 (5th Cir. 1991), n.217
United States v. Spilotro, 786 F.2d 808 (8th Cir. 1986), n.9
United States v. Steinhorn, 927 F.2d 195 (4th Cir. 1991), n.234
United States v. Stricklin, 932 F.2d 1353 (10th Cir. 1991), n.88
United States v. Suppa, 799 F.2d 115 (3d Cir. 1986), nn.88, 124
United States v. Swanquist, 125 F.3d 573 (7th Cir. 1997), n.17
United States v. Szott, 768 F.2d 159 (7th Cir. 1985), nn.10, 14
United States v. Temple, 918 F.2d 134 (10th Cir. 1990), n.282
United States v. Torres, 86 F.3d 1029 (11th Cir. 1996), n.182
United States v. Torres, 929 F.2d 291 (7th Cir. 1991), nn.26, 33, 122
United States v. Tortora, 922 F.2d 880 (1st Cir. 1990), nn.9, 17, 19, 25, 157, 184, 200, 201, 202
United States v. Townsend, 897 F.2d 989 (9th Cir. 1990), nn.26, 204
United States v. Traitz, 807 F.2d 322 (3d Cir. 1986), n.203
United States v. Trosper, 809 F.2d 1107 (5th Cir. 1987), n.99
United States v. Troxell, 887 F.2d 830 (7th Cir. 1989), n.270
United States v. Turner, 367 F. Supp. 2d 319 (E.D.N.Y. 2005), nn.146, 150
United States v. Vaccaro, 51 F.3d 189 (9th Cir. 1995), n.178
United States v. Vachon, 869 F.2d 653 (1st Cir. 1989), n.168
United States v. Valenzuela-Verdigo, 815 F.2d 1011 (5th Cir. 1987), n.71
United States v. Valera-Elizondo, 761 F.2d 1020 (5th Cir. 1985), nn.223, 234, 241
United States v. Vance, 851 F.2d 166 (6th Cir. 1988), nn.210, 212
United States v. Vargas, 925 F.2d 1260 (10th Cir. 1991), n.5
United States v. Vargas, 804 F.2d 157 (1st Cir. 1986), nn.88, 107, 111–13
United States v. Vasquez, 113 F.3d 383 (2d Cir. 1977), n.259
United States v. Vega, 483 F.3d. 801 (7th Cir. 2006), n.183
United States v. Volksen, 766 F.2d 190 (5th Cir. 1985), n.46
United States v. Vortis, 785 F.2d 327 (D.C. Cir. 1986), nn.38, 40, 141
United States v. Warneke, 199 F.3d 906 (7th Cir. 1999), n.166
United States v. Welsand, 993 F.2d 1366 (8th Cir. 1993), n.7
United States v. Westbrook, 780 F.2d 1185 (5th Cir. 1986), n.141
United States v. Wheeler, 795 F.2d 839 (9th Cir. 1986), nn.17, 226, 227
United States v. Williams, 788 F.2d 1213 (6th Cir. 1986), n.271
United States v. Williams, 753 F.2d 329 (4th Cir. 1985), n.41
United States v. Wilson, 503 U.S. 329 (1992), nn.273–75
United States v. Winsor, 785 F.2d 755 (9th Cir. 1986), nn.34, 125

The Bail Reform Act of 1984

United States v. Wong-Alvarez, 779 F.2d 583 (11th Cir. 1985), n.11
United States v. Xulam, 84 F.3d 441 (D.C. Cir. 1996), n.40
Waller v. Georgia, 467 U.S. 39 (1984), n.128
Weaver v. United States, 37 F.3d 1411 (9th Cir. 1994), n.269

The Federal Judicial Center

Board

The Chief Justice of the United States, *Chair*
Judge Bernice B. Donald, U.S. District Court for the Western District of Tennessee
Judge Terence T. Evans, U.S. Court of Appeals for the Seventh Circuit
Magistrate Judge Karen Klein, U.S. District Court for the District of North Dakota
Judge James A. Parker, U.S. District Court for the District of New Mexico
Judge Stephen Raslavich, U.S. Bankruptcy Court for the Eastern District of Pennsylvania
Judge Sarah S. Vance, U.S. District Court for the Eastern District of Louisiana
Judge Karen J. Williams, U.S. Court of Appeals for the Fourth Circuit
James C. Duff, Director of the Administrative Office of the U.S. Courts

Director
Judge Barbara J. Rothstein

Deputy Director
John S. Cooke

About the Federal Judicial Center

The Federal Judicial Center is the research and education agency of the federal judicial system. It was established by Congress in 1967 (28 U.S.C. §§ 620–629), on the recommendation of the Judicial Conference of the United States.

By statute, the Chief Justice of the United States chairs the Center's Board, which also includes the director of the Administrative Office of the U.S. Courts and seven judges elected by the Judicial Conference.

The organization of the Center reflects its primary statutory mandates. The Education Division plans and produces education and training programs for judges and court staff, including satellite broadcasts, video programs, publications, curriculum packages for in-court training, and Web-based programs and resources. The Research Division examines and evaluates current and alternative federal court practices and policies. This research assists Judicial Conference committees, who request most Center research, in developing policy recommendations. The Center's research also contributes substantially to its educational programs. The two divisions work closely with two units of the Director's Office—the Systems Innovations & Development Office and Communications Policy & Design Office—in using print, broadcast, and on-line media to deliver education and training and to disseminate the results of Center research. The Federal Judicial History Office helps courts and others study and preserve federal judicial history. The International Judicial Relations Office provides information to judicial and legal officials from foreign countries and assesses how to inform federal judicial personnel of developments in international law and other court systems that may affect their work.

www.ingramcontent.com/pod-product-compliance
Lightning Source LLC
Chambersburg PA
CBHW080717190526
45169CB00006B/2414